US Navy Divers:

BOHICA

by

Dan Fredrickson

PerrierPress

www.PerrierPress.com

Printed in the United States of America

Library of Congress Cataloging-in-Publication Data

ISBN 0-9620177-2-8

Cartoon and cover design by Jerry Fuchs

Table of Contents

Chapter 1

Introduction

1976: The United States Navy was going through one of the most difficult transitions in its history. Vietnam was over, and many conflicting social forces were colliding. Beards were now legal in Navy dress code and more liberal rules of conduct were being explored. Women were serving in positions not before allowed. Stateside, free love, hippies, flower power, and Woodstock promoted a relaxed attitude towards drugs and other intoxicants and these attitudes affected all Naval personnel worldwide. And, for the sailors coming back from Vietnam, serious drug and alcohol problems had suddenly infiltrated Naval ranks. These were problems on a scale that the Navy had never experienced before.

When old-time Navy personnel struggled against these new radical changes happening around them, some of the absurdities of Naval life were revealed. But, a kinder, gentler, politically correct, and sensitive set of rules was being imposed by the new-order government types, who now controlled the Navy. These new ways were being forced down the throats of the crusty old, knuckle-dragging Navy lifers. It was a changing of the guard then, and many of the older generation were forced out, kicking and screaming. Some of them were buried along the way, not able to change, or refusing to leave when their time was over.

I encountered many of these career old timers and many of the stories in this book tell how hard Navy life had become for them. It was a matter of the survival of the fittest and, as a deep sea diver, I was determined to survive.

This book is about my experiences in 1976 as a Navy diver on board the USS Puget Sound, as we all lived through this transition, attempting to flow past one road block after another. All the stories are true. All the characters are real however, their names have been changed to protect the guilty. I tried to tell each incident exactly as I remembered it. And, just remember, your tax dollars paid for it all.

Chapter 2

Taking The Plunge

People would ask me why I joined the Navy and I would answer that I wanted to be a diver. I'd checked out all the commercial diving schools and thought the Navy offered a better and safer training program. I made it sound like I'd taken a lot of time to think and weigh the differences, and to come to this logical conclusion. But the truth was, I decided on the spur of the moment to join the Navy, out of fear of living a 9-to-5 life. This life would have been easy, with little or no adventure, and very disappointing in the end.

I was going to college and getting decent grades and was on the wrestling team and partying a lot with my friends. I sat around one afternoon, and thought, "Is this all there is for me?" The next day I enlisted.

I'd wanted to be a diver since I was a kid and I had two macho man heroes in my life who motivated me to go for it. The Number One Hero was my Uncle Raymond, a 30-year Marine, sports star, and all-around determined tough-as-nails guy. He was always someone I could talk to about everything. He never told me I was stupid for some of the dumb and dangerous things I did. He always seemed to ask the perfect question in response to a question I asked, so I could figure the answer out for myself.

"Uncle Raymond, what would you do when you had Japs all around you shooting, and guys dropping, and no relief coming?"

"What do think would be the worst thing you could do?" Uncle Raymond responded.

After thinking for a few seconds I answered, "Freak out?"

Uncle Raymond quickly countered, "Which is another word for........?"

"Panic?"

"Correct! That's the worst thing of all. It got more guys killed then just about anything else. Now, what would be the next thing after that, if you were me?"

Again I pictured the whole scenario, something my uncle experienced many, many times, earning him six Silver Stars, (one step below the Medal of Honor), four Navy Crosses, four Purple Hearts, and many other minor awards. He'd been nominated for the Medal of Honor six times yet received the Silver Stars instead. He attributed it to a commanding officer that was a pussy and in disfavor with command head quarters who didn't have enough guts to push it through. Thus, politics is also involved in heroism awards.

I thought up another answer to Uncle Raymond's question for a question.

"Make a decision and go with it, with everything you have."

"That's right. Sometimes you still need to be flexible, because of changing circumstances, but some kind of action must be taken. Remember though, sometimes the best action is to do nothing at all," he would say.

These two lessons were repeated in my head, over and over, and helped me many times during the high stress periods of dive school.

I'd always liked to hear about my uncle's tales of being in China on a gunboat in the early 1930s, like the movie, The Sand Pebbles with Steve McQueen. Traveling and having adventures like my uncle was the main reason for my joining the Navy. I'd never wanted to be a mindless robot like a Marine (I never told my uncle that), but seeing the world, meeting exotic women and having fun – like my recruiter told me I would – convinced me to sign on the dotted line.

I never consulted my parents or friends about my decision, because I didn't want to hear how stupid I was. I also didn't want to hear from my parents about finishing college and becoming an officer. So, I didn't tell anyone until after I'd signed up and was scheduled to leave, at end of the school year.

I decided that since I was now legally an adult, I'd make my own decisions. Then, if things didn't work out, I'd have no one to blame but myself. That way I'd set my own career path much the same way Uncle Raymond did.

My second macho hero was Lloyd Bridges who starred as Mike Nelson in the television show Sea Hunt. I'd asked for a scuba mask for Christmas when I was five years old so I could pretend to be Mike Nelson in the bathtub. I was a diver from then on. Even at five, I could swim well, since I had taken lessons and was a natural water bug.

I never missed a Sea Hunt program and was in awe of how Mike Nelson was always able to cut the air hose of the bad guys. Later, I learned as a diver, that they were actually cutting the exhaust hose on the double-hose regulator. Mike Nelson never killed anyone because he was just too cool to do that. He vanquished foreign spies and smugglers and - my favorite - caught the horrible drug dealers who grew a new strain of underwater marijuana. "You know they sell this stuff to little kids," Mike Nelson proclaimed indignantly. It was my favorite show and those lines were often repeated by me many times, partying with my diver friends. Whatever Mike Nelson said, it must be true, and I took it as gospel. The adventure and mystery under the water always fascinated me, and Lloyd Bridges will never know how much he influenced my life through a fictional character.

Thinking of these two men, one real and one fantasy, guided me to roll the dice and take a chance on the Navy. Becoming a deep sea diver was my ultimate goal in life, and I made it happen.

Chapter 3

Returning Victorious To The Ship

Standing at the front of the pier, I looked at the destroyer tender USS Puget Sound that was tied securely to it. I had just returned after successfully completing Second Class Deep Sea Diving School – a school that defeated nine out of the last 10 sailors from our ship who even qualified to enter.

Mixed emotions ran through me. I'd been on board the ship more than a year as a turd-chasing hull technician, and that was one of the worst experiences of my life – working for an alcoholic, redneck, mean-spirited Chief who hated himself and tried his best to make everyone else around him feel as bad as he did. He especially hated California surfer-boy types. If I had not been accepted for diving school, I had seriously considered going AWOL – just to get away from this asshole, my scummy job, and the entire US Navy.

I had vowed that I was either going to pass diving school or die trying. There was no middle ground. That was the attitude I had when I left the ship. I had burned all my bridges behind me.

As I stood on the pier, wearing my new green uniform and proudly wearing my dive pin, I realized just how great it was going to come back onboard and to shove my dive pin into the faces of all the assholes who told me I'd never make it. I didn't think that my chest could puff up more than it had now.

I remembered I had once kept the acceptance orders a secret until the day I was supposed to check off the ship. That way, I wouldn't get any grief from my division officer, Lt. Larry (Hemorrhoid) Bunzy, and Chief (Hangover) Hartford. With my checkoff sheet in hand, I had to get the chain of command to sign me out. I thought about forging the whole sheet, but I was worried that my two worst enemies would investigate how I got off the ship without their signatures and they would then get me kicked out of diving school. I couldn't take that chance. I played it by the book. I handed the check-out sheet to the alcoholic Chief who snarled at me.

"You've got duty today. I won't sign this until tomorrow. You have to stand your watches."

Chief knew no one would be in the personnel office on Saturday and my first day of diving class started on Monday. I had to get his signature immediately. I spoke to him in a respectful and controlled way.

"I'll stand my duty, Chief, but the personnel chief said I needed to get this back by 1400. So sign it and I'll stand my watches and check out tomorrow," I lied.

"I'm the duty chief, so you better be there at 1600 hours or your ass is mine. Got that?"

"Sure Chief. Thanks."

He signed the paper and threw it at me. Next hurdle was the Hemorrhoid. He'd gotten his nickname from the scar that ran between his eyes, all the way to the back of his head. He'd been a helicopter pilot in Vietnam and was shot down and hit with a piece of the helicopter's blade. It peeled his scalp back and took part of his skull with it. He had a metal plate in his head and a scar as a reminder of the incident. At first, he was known as butt-head, because the scar looked like a butt crack on his head. Then, because he became such a pain around the shop, he became known as Hemorrhoid Head which was naturally shortened to just Hemorrhoid.

Hemorrhoid was a hyperactive guy who hated his job as Engineering Hull Division officer. He wanted to fly helicopters again but he was no longer physically qualified as a pilot. He had 14 years already in the Navy and was committed to serving out a 20-year career path. He still got headaches, on a daily basis, from his accident and was very emotionally volatile and unpredictable. It was impossible for any of us to guess what kind of a mood he'd be in. He could be one of the guys, hanging out in the shop, telling stories, or he could swing to the other side and be a vindictive asshole, ready to jump on you for any slight reason. And the worst part was that there was no pattern to his headache moods.

I needed Hemorrhoid's signature next to check off the Puget Sound. I walked into the Damage Control Central where his office was. I was hoping he was in a good mood, but he had just gotten off the telephone with Chief Hangover.

"So, you think you're checking out today? You'll stand your duty," he said with a nasty curl of his lips.

"I already told the Chief that I'd do that, but the Personnel Chief needs this by 1400 hours to process it today," I again lied.

Hemorrhoid miraculously believed me as well, and signed my checkoff sheet. I quickly got the rest of the people whose signatures I needed. When I finally turned my completed paper to the personnel office, I stood there anxiously waiting as my paperwork was processed without a glitch. Finally the Personnel Chief handed me my envelope with my orders.

"Am I officially off the ship now?" I cautiously asked the Chief.

"Yup. Get your gear and get out of here sailor. Good luck," he said, waving a pleasant good-by.

"Thanks," I said, and out the door I went, feeling 10 pounds lighter. I had already packed my stuff and it was sitting on my bunk with my green duffel bag. With orders in hand, I headed for the quarterdeck to leave the ship. I showed both orders and ID card and asked permission to leave the ship. Saluting the quarterdeck watch, I walked down the brow. I had never been happier in my entire life. I was free – relatively speaking, anyway.

Going to diving school was the reason I'd joined the Navy. It took me two years of bullshit to finally get my chance. Now it was do or die. I felt confident that I was going to make it. Walking down the pier to where my car was parked, I heard my name yelled from the ship. I looked up and there, standing on the fantail of the ship smoking a cigarette, was Chief Hangover Hartford.

"Where the fuck do you think you're going? You got duty. Get your fucking ass back here now!"

Waving my orders in the air in a mock farewell, I put on my best smile and yelled back. "I'm checked off. Hey, fuck you, too!" I said as I shot him the bird and laughed. I kept walking down the pier.

"You'll be back, and you'll be mine, you fucking asshole. You'll never make it, you fucking loser," he screamed behind me. If I needed any additional incentive to pass diving school, it was just given to me.

Now was the moment I was returning victorious to the Puget Sound. Seeing me in greens with a dive pin was going to twist Hangover and Hemorrhoid into pieces – and they both would not be able to do anything about it. I was now away from their control. I felt elated, energized, and eager to confront all the jerks who never had any confidence in me. The moment was mine. I had earned it!

The USS Puget Sound AD 38 was a destroyer tender, which is nothing more than a floating repair ship. It was the next-largest ship to an aircraft carrier and usually had a crew between 1,300 and 1,600 sailors, which varied depending if the ship was going on deployment or not. The crew could do just about every conceivable repair right on the ship from photo lab work, metal and plastic work, electronics repair, and parts molding and machining, to engine and motor repair, sewing, and anything else that was needed. The diving locker, where I was now assigned, was in the R-1 Repair Division. The shops here included the welding, pipefitting, sheet metal, and carpentry divisions in addition to the divers' area.

I strutted around the ship in my new green uniform. The first stop before going to the dive locker was the Hull Technician shop to make sure Chief Hangover Hartford got a good look at me. I had been gone four months and there were a few new faces here, but most of them were the same guys I'd worked with for more than a year. To the man, none of them thought I would pass diving school. Pulling out a piece of paper, I walked in and started calling out names around the shop.

"Foster, $20. Haines, $10. Wilson, $10. Jimbo, $20. All right you mother-fuckers, cough up the dough and kiss the fucking dive pin."

I cleaned up. Before I left, bets had been placed that I'd fail and be back in the shop. Seeing me standing at the hatch, dressed in the diver's uniform and sporting a diver's pin, the commotion started.

"Wow! The fucker actually made it!"

"That's great!"

"Congratulations!!"

"Wait – til Hangover sees you!"

"Speaking of Hangover," I inquired, "where is the asshole?"

"He went to D.C. Central, but he'll be back soon. Man, you really did something to him when you left. For days – no, weeks – all he could do was go on about how he was going to fuck you over when you got back. He'd go up to personnel every week to see if you had flunked out and you could just tell by looking at him what the news was," said

Hull Technician Fireman Foster.

"Ya, all we had to say was, 'I heard Fredrickson's doing great in diving school,' or 'We heard that Fredrickson was top of his class.' Even though we didn't know anything, that was enough to set him off again. I think the guy's on about a case of Maalox a day. And with you back, this will get him up to two cases a day," laughed Hull Technician Third Class Haines.

"Seeing me will make his day. Foster, go get your Polaroid and I'll sit in his chair with my feet on his desk. When he sees my little momento," pointing to my dive pin, "we're talking cardiac arrest. He'll flip harder than the time I repaired the head and grinned at him. Remember that time?"

The whole group flashed back on the night I had passively stood there, confrontationally grinning at Hangover, embarrassing him in front of his crew, despite the fact that he was drunk as a skunk. That night had permanently set the Chief against me forever!

That was back when the ship was docked in Naples, Italy, and it was during one of my duty nights on my first cruise on the Puget Sound. One of the berthing heads (bathrooms) had a leaking water pipe. At 2 a.m., two other men and I attempted to weld the leak shut, but the cutoff valves wouldn't completely shut the water off. Rather than wake up 60 chiefs at this hour in the morning, we decided to secure the head and repair it properly when everyone was up and the successive cutoff valves could be turned off. This was the way the repair job could be done properly.

It just so happened that this was Chief Hangover's berthing head and he came in drunk, as usual, ready to unload his filled-up bladder. When he saw the sign on the door, "SECURED," he went berserk, storming down to the engineer's berthing, turning the lights on 150 sleeping guys, and screaming for the hull technicians to get up and muster in the shop. He was so drunk that he couldn't remember where any of his men slept, so all of them pulled the covers over their heads and hid.

Fortunately, the Master-at-Arms – the ship's security guard – heard the commotion and came down to find out what was going on. Seeing the drunk Chief, he asked him to leave or be taken to the Master-at-Arms office. As he stumbled out, Chief drunkenly bellowed, "I know all you motherfuckers are awake. I'll see you in the morning, you can bet your fucking asses." He staggered up the stairs to his berthing, followed by the MAA.

The morning muster was a real scene. Hangover was hungover to the max and had the most evil scowl on his face. He had one front tooth that stuck out farther than the others and it always hung out over his lower lip. This made him look like he had even more of a permanent scowl on his lips. Chief Hangover walked to the center of the shop, surrounded by his troops. He held the paper sign that had been attached to the door of the head.

"Who the fuck had duty last night?" he screamed, shaking the paper violently.

No one stepped forward to claim the honor, so he railed on. "I'll find out soon enough and their fucking asses will be mine!" His face was turning almost scarlet and spit shot out between his mismatched teeth. "And when I find out who did this, I'm going to kick his ass." He circled around the room looking closely in the face of each sailor, making sure each one took him seriously. "Those responsible better be ready to shit themselves, the stupid motherfuckers," he railed. Peering face to face with each of his crew, he kept ranting about their incompetence and laziness, getting more and more worked up, walking faster and faster in circles, until he stopped dead at what he saw peering back at him. Me.

There I was, standing at attention and staring back at him with my best, widest grin on my face. This was not a smirk, but an ear-to-ear smile; the kind of smile that says "your authority means nothing to me and I have absolutely no respect for you." I kept eye contact with him and didn't look down. Chief Hangover read my smile with perfect accuracy.

"You wrote this piece of shit, didn't you, you California faggot motherfucker," he screamed with a voice that seemed to rip out the back of his throat.

I continued to smile, maybe even wider. The guys in the shop were paralyzed with shock at what was going on.

"You keep smiling you faggot motherfucker and I'll wipe that son-of-a-bitch smile off your stupid face!" He was out of control – completely hysterical now. "I'll crack your fucking skull!" He moved in on me like he was going to physically attack me.

I stood my ground, smiling, but ready to move at a moment's notice if he made a further move towards me. Luckily, HT-1 Campbell jumped in front of Chief Hangover and yelled,"Chief, we need to go outside, right now!" Holding on to the Chief, who was still yelling, "I'll part your hair, you motherfucker" (along with many other variations on this theme), the guys pulled him through the door and out onto the fantail to try to get him under control. After they were gone, the guys left inside the shop went wild.

"I can't believe you did that!"

"I thought it was a fight for sure!"

"Hangover's head almost exploded this time!"

Everyone was laughing and thanking God it wasn't them the Chief was going to have a lifelong vendetta against.

After the Chief calmed down some hours later, and after a nap which lowered the blood alcohol level in his system, he decided to put me on report for "dereliction of duty," and "disrespect of a Superior Petty Officer." I knew something like that would happen, and was one step ahead of him. I checked the Uniform Code of Military Justice manual and had report chits written up on the Chief for "attempted assault," and for "expressing a threat," and, to add fuel to the fire, "drunk on duty," even though I couldn't actually prove it legally.

Chief Hangover Hartford was now faced with counter charges and when HT-1 Campbell explained to him the legitimate reason why the head was closed for repairs, Hangover knew he would end up with the short end of the stick. The California faggot had made the entire shop laugh at him and he couldn't do anything about it. It was two miserable months later that I received my orders to report to diving school.

Standing now before these same guys in the shop, we collectively reminisced about the smiling incident that almost pushed Hangover too far.

"I'd better do some smiling exercises so I don't pull a cheek muscle smiling at Hangover when he comes back. What do you think?" I asked the shop guys. I went through exaggerated face contortions and lip and cheek stretching and whinnying like a horse to loosen my facial muscles. I let my face snap back to that same big insolent smile that almost caused the Chief's heart to stop. Everyone in the shop was doubled up with laughter.

"I don't know what it is, but every time I think of Hangover, my face automatically gets like this. Think I should go to medical? No. I know what they'll tell me: 'You have a case of in-your-face-asshole-itis.' And what's the cure, doc? 'Laugh two times in Hartford's face every four hours and call me in the morning.'" They were rolling on the floor.

"What the fuck is going on in here?" yelled Chief Hangover Hartford as he stormed into the shop unexpectedly.

Snapping to attention, I saluted the Chief and announced, "Hull Technician Third Class, Second Class Diver Fredrickson reporting back to the ship." I then looked around like I was lost. "Oh my gosh. I don't work here anymore. That's right, I'm in Repair Division Dive Locker now. Nice seeing you again, Chief."

Chief Hangover Hartford's face contorted and turned a shade of purple, his mind was still sluggish from last night's drinking, but his head was definitely going to explode. I continued, "I know it's an emotional moment for you, Chief, with me coming back to see you and all, so I'll just head to my new job in the Dive Locker in Repair Division!!" I headed for the door, wiggling my hips and wearing my best insolent smile. Hartford stood speechless, with his fists clinched and his jaw squeezing his teeth so hard you could hear them grinding and crumbling. I left him in this condition.

I went out into the cargo handling passageway to the dive locker and stood outside the door excitedly. I had now fulfilled one of my life's dreams, to be a deep sea diver. I took a deep breath to relax and opened the door, walking into a very new and different part of the Navy.

Chapter 4

Baby Diver

As I slowly entered the door, I saw all the guys sitting around the shop.

"Hey, look who finally showed up. It's our new baby diver," announced HT-3 Chip Chance.

I had always held divers in awe, attaching godlike status to them. All sailors did. Navy divers were definitely at the top of the ship's pecking order. They were the men. They were kings. They had ass-kicking reputations. Even though a lot of it was rumor, kept alive by the divers themselves, enough was the truth, which kept their tough-guy image alive and thriving. Now, I was one of them. I was on the top of the heap. I felt good about myself – the best I ever have.

They all clustered around me, introducing themselves and "inspecting" me. There was HT Third Class Jerry West, Boatswain Mate First Class Edward Benunni, HT Second Class Patrick Shea, HT Fireman Tim Workman, HT Third Class Chip Chance, and the boss, Machinist Mate Senior Chief John Ludwig. They all congratulated me and offered me a seat. I was instantly made to feel a welcomed part of the group. This was the first time I felt I belonged anywhere since I had joined the Navy two years ago. The Senior Chief was even supportive and appeared genuinely glad to have me in the group. I mentally compared him to Hangover and Hemorrhoid.

"I'm glad you made it through. You're the first one to get the pin in over two years. The last ones were Chance and West. We've probably sent more than 10 guys, and you finally succeeded," said Senior Chief Ludwig, shaking my hand.

The boss had welcomed me. I knew that my life would no longer be an hourly and daily fight for survival against my superior officers. There were good guys in the Navy after all. This was going to be a real team.

I was given no time to settle in. Divers dive and that's what we were going to do.

"I think we need to get this new baby diver some experience with us, don't ya think?" said Benunni.

"Okay. Get Fredrickson some equipment and let's go," ordered Senior Chief Ludwig.

They brought me a wet suit, booties, gloves and fins and we all headed for the dive boat. I was told to drive. Although I had driven several boats before, I had no experience with the 40' fiberglass style that was used as the dive boat. It had a low, front cabin that stepped down on the starboard side into the cabin below with a steering wheel on the port side of the main deck area. Benunni gave me the run-down on how to drive the boat, talking to me as if I were a five year old.

"This is the steering wheel. It turns left. It turns right. And, it goes straight. This is the shifting lever. It goes forward and it goes backward." He demonstrated as he talked. "And right in the middle, it goes nowhere." Benunni thought he was being real cute. "You turn this clockwise, you go fast. You turn this the other way, you go slow. Now push this button and it starts, and this button, and it stops." He walked away from me acting like he had just finished an intensely complex explanation about an extremely difficult operation. "It's all yours now, baby diver. You break it, you fix it."

I started the boat and perfectly pulled out of the very tight mooring berth. They were all hoping to make good–hearted fun out of my incompetence. My previous experience with power boats and sailing made this one rather easy to control. I was directed to pull up to the Fast Frigate USS Farragut, park the dive boat alongside it, and did so with no problem.

"The baby diver's no fun at all. In fact, he drives better than Benunni," Chance teased.

"Maybe the baby diver should give you driving lessons, Benunni," said the Senior Chief.

Benunni gave his standard, all-inclusive answer when he had no comeback at all. "Fuck all of you!"

Everyone was laughing and getting ready to dive. I was excited and nervous because this was my first working dive and I wanted to do a quality job. The diving hoses were on a rack that was pulled up on a hinge from the afterhold. In that hold there were two high–pressure flasks, 10'x2' wide, which supplied the divers with their primary and secondary air. Each flask held 3,000 psi of air and could support two divers for about eight hours under water, depending on the depth. The flasks were connected to an air distribution manifold that reduced the air pressure to the proper flow for the depth of the divers. There was a chart on the bulkhead next to the adjustable pressure–reducing valve and a gauge, so no one had to figure out pressure mathematically. This was about as sailor–proof as it could get.

We were diving with a Jack Brown band mask, a full-face mask held on by five adjustable rubber straps that looked like a spider on the back of the head. On the side of the mask was a hoke valve, which was a simple on/off twist valve. The air was adjusted by turning the handle clockwise for less, and counterclockwise for more. The mask was connected with a hose and safety wire, which attached to a belt worn around the waist. There was no form of communicating with those above the water other than with line pull signals. This was all the equipment included in the simplest Navy diving rig.

I suited up in my wet suit, booties and gloves and sat on the bench next to the hoses to receive my instructions and to hear the emergency procedures. This was going to be my first solo working dive. Chance was the standby diver. My first job was to find and inspect the port screw, rudder and shaft. Finding them wasn't as easy as it sounded. I looked into the chocolate–brown water and saw a thousand jellyfish floating all over the surface. There was trash and fluffy brown foam filling in the gaps. If this wasn't disgusting enough, there was a turd floating where I was about to enter the water.

The visibility was about one to two feet with a light, after three feet of depth. They gave me the Jack Brown mask and I adjusted the straps and the air flow, gave the okay sign, and stood on the edge of the boat ready to enter the filthy water.

"Hit it!" said the Senior Chief.

I took a deep breath and stepped over the side hitting the water in the standard entry, with one leg forward and one leg back in a scissors kicking motion, which kept me upright and my head out of the water. Once in the water, adjusting to the cold temperature, I looked up to see that all the divers on the boat were scoring the quality of my water entry like a high dive contest.

"5.5 too much arch in the back and the head tilted to the side."

"6.0 small leg splash, but left arm was too wide and head went down too deep."

I smiled and started to swim over to the USS Farragut when I received the hose line pull signal to stop. They were signaling me back to the dive boat. I swam back and came close to the rear exit ladder when my hose and safety line were pulled tight, pinning me against the ladder. I couldn't move my legs up to climb the ladder because they were hooked under the last ladder rung and I couldn't push my chest out enough to get room to come up either. Looking up, I saw four smiling faces and four exposed cocks starting to pee on me.

I couldn't go up or down. I was trapped and held tight against the ladder. The yellow rain fell on me as I pretended to enjoy the whole experience. Finally, they let me go. As I swam away in the direction of the ship, I heard them shouting at me.

"You are now baptized in the name of the sea, and the diving community. Fredrickson is good to the last drop."

I gave the signal that I was going down and the Senior Chief waved me to start. No wonder those guys were drinking so much coffee before we got on the dive boat. As I started down, I noticed how sound perception changed underwater. I could hear muffled machinery running from the Farragut and water moving all around me. Visibility was gone, even with the light after five feet of depth, and there was a lot of junk in the water bumping against my body. The worst things were the jellyfish. I couldn't see them, but I could feel them. In some spots it felt like I was swimming through loose Jello.

Everywhere that water entered my wet suit it felt like fire from the jellyfish tentacles which surrounded me. The stinging pain became so distracting that I was almost ready to abort the dive. But, I knew this was not the way to end my first solo dive in front of this new and very important group of guys. I concentrated and tried to shut off the pain from my mind to attend to the tasks I had to complete. I managed to find the screw and go through all the steps of inspection and then went to the other components as well. When finished, I gave my line signals that I was coming up, and proceeded to the surface.

Swimming back to the dive boat, I handed the plastic slate with all the measurements and inspection information to the Chief, who looked at the figures and said, "I want you to go down and check the dunce cap screws." I gave him the okay and swam back to the side of the Farragut again.

Giving the proper line signals, I dove down and found the screw. The dunce cap was the cover over the big nut that held on the screw to the shaft. The cover was attached to the propeller by several small screws that needed to be checked regularly. Just as I was ready to go to work, I received a signal on my hose to pull in a square mark. This is a rope or line tied to the hose and is used to transfer items to and from the surface. "I must have forgotten something," I thought, and started to pull in the line. Hand over hand in the blackness of the water surrounding me, suddenly my hand hit something. I grabbed my light, which was tied to my wrist with a small line. Turning it towards the square mark I saw, neatly tied in a bundle, was my freshly starched and pressed, new green uniform and jungle boots.

At first I was really pissed, but then I pictured all those assholes laughing on the boat. My next thought was how I was going to get even with them. Giving the signal to come up, I proceeded to the surface. Their voices pierced the surface even before I did.

"That beautiful pair of greens just couldn't bare to be away from you and just had to swim after you."

"The uniform did a better water entry than you did."

I just smiled and sat on the bench and stripped out of my wet suit. The Chief came over and looked at me and said, "Those jellyfish stings look real bad. Are you okay?"

"They hurt a lot. It feels like fire or acid or something," I foolishly admitted.

Chance approached me real concerned, "Does it hurt the baby diver real bad?"

"Ya. Stings like hell."

"We've got some stuff to put on it that will kill the pain quick. Do you want to try it?

Eager to have the pain stop, I enthusiastically said, "Sure."

The divers grabbed me and threw me down on the deck and held my arms and legs and proceeded to piss all over my ankles and wrists. I started to struggle when Chance started to pee towards my neck, which was stung very badly.

"Hey turkey, you keep moving and I might piss all over your face," Chance warned, letting the stream flow over my neck.

I stopped moving immediately, as Chance and then West, started peeing all over my neck. Finally after an eternity, they finished and let go of my legs and arms. I didn't know what to do and just sat there. Do I laugh it off or start swinging at the grinning faces all around me?

"Well, how does it feel?" Chance asked in a mock-serious tone.

To my amazement, the pain was almost gone and the bright red sting marks were now turning light pink and fading as I watched.

"Do you think we piss on you because we like to?" Chance added. "We were just trying to help you. We won't do it again because you seem to enjoy it too much. We've heard about you California boys. Don't want you getting stung on purpose just to get the treatment again."

What a first day I had. Lording it over Chief Hangover, meeting my new diving team, getting pissed on twice, diving in slime water, stung to all hell by jellyfish – I was exhausted. God, being a deep sea diver turned out to be everything I ever dreamed it would be – and even better! I loved being a diver!

Chapter 5

Benunni - The Most Disgusting Man to Walk the Earth

BM1 Edward Benunni was a 5'6" Italian pit bull. He weighed 190 pounds, had no neck, and a very large head. He was also known as Stinky, but never to his face. There were legitimate reasons for giving him this nickname.

There were times when what we dived in was nothing more than sewage. Ships dispelled their sewage holding tanks directly into the sea and, if moored, dumped the sewage directly into the harbor. The sewage then floated around the perimeter of the ship until the tides changed and took it far out to sea. Because we made underwater repairs to the ship's hull, we had to frequently dive and work in these cesspools. After a long day of diving in brown water, filled with turds and garbage, we scrubbed and sterilize ourselves fanatically – but not Benunni. Not Stinky! If he did take a shower, it was called a Marine–type shower; wet in, wet out, and no soap ever. Benunni acted like he'd melt if soap touched his body.

About halfway into the last cruise, there were so many complaints about the smell from his coffin locker bed in the berthing area that Senior Chief Ludwig had to inspect it. Senior Chief nearly gagged from the odor that emanated from the coffin locker after he opened it. He ordered Benunni to wash and sterilize everything in it and to stand by for inspections every week for the rest of the cruise.

Now, Benunni was an excellent diver and could also drive just about any kind of craft on the water or under it, from an aircraft carrier to a submersible craft. He had even passed his Coast Guard licensing test for tugboat captain. He loved to critique everyone's boat–driving techniques and no one was ever up to his standards. He questioned the boat driver on the rules of the road, on boat safety, and on old–time Navy trivia. If the rules of the road, safety, or trivia questions weren't answered correctly, the offending sailor received "The Benunni Lecture". Everyone had the wording down by heart now.

"Sailors of today have no respect for tradition and history. When I was a young sailor, etc., etc., etc." It could go on and on, depending on how badly the offending sailor screwed up. Everyone bitched about all the questions and grilling we got, but we had to admit we learned a lot, and we didn't forget either – like we would ever let him know, though.

Benunni volunteered for Master-at-Arms duty for the upcoming cruise because he was tired of diving everyday and MAAs really didn't work very hard. He was having a serious case of the lazies and wanted an easy job for the upcoming deployment.

Benunni had the profound ability to fart at will – not your standard stinker, but the something-crawled-up-your-ass-and-died kind of fart that left a rainbow haze in the light. If you were caught in the vicinity of one of these major farts, you would have experienced biological warfare at its worst. Benunni, himself, told us this story after he had returned from leave.

He was shopping with his wife for furniture and was being dragged from store to store for over three hours, trying to find the perfect bedroom end tables. He was fed up with it. While she was talking to the salesperson, he wandered off into a smaller room of furniture displays. After looking around to see if he was alone, he let loose a bomb. This was a 10+ on the Benunni fart scale, and he was proud of this baby. In a few seconds, his wife walked into the display area, looking for him.

"God, Ed!" was all she said with disgust. Before she could leave the area, the salesman came in and the smell hit him too. With a very serious face, Benunni said to his wife, "Honey, couldn't you wait till you got outside?" Needless to say, the shopping trip ended right there. His wife didn't talk to him for a week. Benunni claimed it was the best week of his life.

As an ex-diver, and a new Master-at-Arms, Benunni's favorite part of the job was lecturing the sailors who got busted for smoking pot on how stupid they were, as they mustered for their evening of extra duty assignments. This was part of their punishment along with the loss of one rank and restriction to the ship. "I just love this part of my job so much. It makes me feel so-o-o-o good to assign you stupid mother-fuckers this extra duty, that I might have to go to the head and relieve myself of this huge hard-on I have." Once that badge was on his chest, he'd routinely cruise down to the dive locker, saying he was just looking for dopers.

"Hey, look who's here, it's Deputy Dog's twin brother, Deputy Hog," I shouted.

"Ya, I'm going to enjoy the day when you fuck up and I catch you smoking your dope. I'll bust your ass so fast, you won't know what hit you," Benunni warned me.

"Then you better sneak up on me down wind. Otherwise, I'll smell your stinky ass a mile away, fat boy," I said.

"I'm patient. I'll have my day. You can count on that," Benunni said smugly.

Benunni came down just to hangout with us. He missed diving people, but he didn't miss getting into the water anymore. He'd been a diver for more than 18 years and was on his last enlistment before retiring. He didn't figure on making Chief, so he resigned himself to using his Tug Boat Captain's license to push ships around the Norfolk area. "Sucking off the government tit, pushing Navy tubs around" he'd say.

Tim Workman entered, pretending he didn't see Benunni there. "Man, I thought the sewage vent had backed up when I opened the door. But I guess you explain the odor," smiling at Benunni.

West chimed in, "Ya, every time I'd see Benunni in the water, he'd prove the Hull Technician's theory that the stinkiest turds always float."

"Ladies, you better reenlist," said Benunni, "and keep your day jobs because your attempts at humor are sad, to say the least. But at least I'm giving you an honest critique, so you don't make total fools of yourself again," Benunni said smugly.

Still smiling, he rocked back on the back legs of his chair. Unfortunately the floor had just been waxed and was very slippery. When he rocked back, the rear legs slid and he fell back, all the way to the floor, whacking his head on the wall. We just let him lay there, stunned. He lay on the floor for a while before he was finally able to get up. The laughter was out of control, and the insults flew.

" I think his middle lard pack shifted aft too fast and sent him down."

"No, no, no, it was too much hot air jetting out of his mouth and he just blew over."

"He probably farted and the chair legs disintegrated."

Benunni set the chair back up and sat down smiling. He was red faced and took it like a man. The look on his face was confident but wily. You could tell that he was thinking, "They'll fuck up sooner or later, and I'll have my day. Just be patient."

Chapter 6

Ship's Open House

We were preparing to leave in two weeks on our scheduled six-month repair rotation in the Mediterranean Sea. On top of these difficult preparations, Captain Horner decided to host a ship's open house for the general public. With all the pressure of stockpiling needed supplies, catching up on the maintenance for our own ship, and getting all the equipment ready for a six-month deployment, an open house was the last thing we needed. Ship's open houses were nothing more than pains in the ass. They were a lot like zone inspections. Everything had to be shined, buffed, and polished because you never knew what civilian bigwigs would be snooping around.

In the dive locker, everything was starting to look real good. The green tile deck was so shiny that the glare from the overhead lights almost hurt your eyes. We also had a spectacular 30-gallon freshwater aquarium which was trimmed out in beautiful walnut and finished to a glossy shine. The aquarium was our pride and joy. It always looked clean and clear, and all of us were very knowledgeable in keeping it that way.

On either side of the aquarium was a Mark 5 deep-sea diving helmet mounted on finished walnut stands. These are the old round brass helmets that have been used by Navy deep sea divers for more than 50 years. These helmets were shined to a beautiful sparkle, and with the aquarium in between, it really took people by surprise when they came into our locker.

Many people would ask how we could have an aquarium when we were at sea. First, the Puget Sound didn't go to sea all that often and when it did, the ship was so large that it didn't rock that much unless there were really big swells. When that happened we would just lower the water level in the aquarium, until it wouldn't splash over. We knew how far to drop the level down and I never saw spillover even during large seas.

A few weeks earlier Benunni, Workman, Nelson, and I were

working on the UDATS underwater video recording system. It had a nasty habit of blinking out the picture and tracking badly every time we would move it around. It really sucked when we were on a job and the camera kept screwing up. This was an ongoing problem with this brand-new video system.

As always, I was the one who would fix technical-type things when they broke. Everyone turned dumb when the electrical stuff didn't work, but they sure were there to critique my work after I was done. I had Benunni looking over my shoulder, giving me his expert high-tech opinion.

"Aren't you done with that thing yet, shit bird? Just whack it hard, right here, and it'll work fine."

"I don't want to hear about your sex life," I countered

"Oh, the sultan of jokes speaks again."

Benunni smacked the side of the recorder unit. Amazingly, the picture straightened up for a while, and then tracked off again. This could only mean one thing: the heads were loose. Once I tightened them, the picture stayed straight. All that needed to be done was to adjust the tracking and bring the picture back to the center of the screen. Benunni started strutting around the dive locker like he was a mechanical genius, taking credit for fixing the video.

"You'd still have your head up your ass trying to figure that thing out if it wasn't for me. Why I'm so-o-o good I could fart on it and probably fix it."

"If you farted anywhere near this machine, the tape would melt," I said. Benunni wasn't listening because he was intent on what Workman was doing – unfolding a life-size Penthouse poster of Miss April.

Everything stopped – like we were all hypnotized – as Miss April was unfurled. She was a beautiful brunette with the right attributes to make any heterosexual sailor drool. We all seriously gawked at Miss April with reverence and respect.

"Wow, is she something or what?" I stammered.

"Yaaah," Nelson breathed out, softly mesmerized at her beauty as his head moved up and down from her tits to between her legs. He looked like a slow-motion bobbing-head doll. With Benunni there, the moment of feminine idolization didn't last long.

"Well, if you guys are so horned out over that slut, why don't you take a picture with her and send it home to your mammas?"

"Oh, shut up, asshole. Your idea of something good looking is a foot-long hot dog about to be crammed into your pie hole," I shouted.

Benunni was from New York City, and therefore was the resident "expert" on how to prepare and eat hot dogs. According to him, everyone else should bow to his unbridled authority on the matter. Hot-dog-ology wasn't something New York City outsiders could learn. He said the knowledge was ingrained in your blood if you were from New York. And that was all that needed to be said.

"Just remember: hot dog, mustard and bun. You can't go wrong, dumb shits. Altogether now: hot dogs, mustard and buns." This was Benunni's hot dog purist theory for true Americans. Anything else was just plain "unpatriotic."

"Is that what you say to your wife when you want sex? Except yours isn't the foot-long kind, it's the mini Frank," I shot back to him. Even Benunni smiled at this.

New Yorkers thought they were experts on anything they knew even a little bit about – and filled in the rest with bull-shit. We learned all about these things from Benunni. His word was New York gospel. Whenever Benunni was proven wrong on a subject, he would just wear you down by getting louder and in your face until you finally didn't want to waste any more time with the stupid matter. Then he would claim victory. "He who lasts, wins", was his motto. "If you were really right," he'd persist, " you'd keep fighting for your opinion to the very end."

Whenever he was in this obnoxious mood, we would take the easy road and tell him that he was the smartest guy in the world, what a joy it was to be in his presence, and that his farts were like roses from heaven. We'd keep up the nice stuff until he finally told us to shut up or he'd leave. We knew how to work him. Benunni was also now interested in examining Miss April's attributes.

"So, why don't you put that poster on the wall over there and we'll see what kind of love making technique you all can try on Miss April. We need to test the UDATS anyway. Might as well have some fun," challenged Benunni.

We all agreed and taped the life-size poster of Miss April on the wall of the dive locker. She was magnificent, laying on a maroon silk bed, wide open for all to see. We all took turns being videotaped and making our best moves on Miss April. From the low-resolution picture on the TV screen, the entire scene looked real. The spell was broken when the Senior Chief barged into the dive locker right after Benunni had brought Miss April to a great orgasm.

"God damn it, get that shit off the wall and let's get moving. We've got to be on the USS California in 30 minutes. That video had better be fixed since you guys have time to be fucking around," he warned and stormed out the door towards the dive boat.

We grabbed the UDATS machine and camera and headed for the dive boat, forgetting about our lovemaking with Miss April.

A couple of days passed and our repair job on the California was complete. The next hurdle was getting through the open house so we could complete preparations for our upcoming deployment to the Mediterranean. Unfortunately, this open house drew the largest crowd of visitors ever. The ship was crawling with people. We had boy scout groups, Admirals' wives, service clubs, a contingent of WWII veterans from the retirement home in Portsmouth. Where did all these civilians come from? And why, in God's name, would they want to spend a few hours on board the USS Puget Sound?

Benunni was the designated guide for our dive locker. He was very good at telling exciting diving tales that kept everyone thrilled, boasting about what macho men deep sea divers were. Most of it was just pure crap, but it made us look good, so what could it hurt?

It was hard not to laugh when he would tell an amazing story with him as the hero – like when he ran out of air underwater, while his small boat squadron was under attack in Vietnam. Pure crap, but the crowd loved it. Hearing his phoney-baloney stories and exaggerations, sometimes we just had to turn away so the people wouldn't see us choking to keep the laughter inside. But being the disciplined group of guys that we were, we kept quiet, biting our tongues.

This open house tour happened to include the Virginia Beach Ladies Auxiliary Club and many of the members were the wives of high ranking officers on board our ship. Some of these women had brought their daughters with them for a tour of daddy's big ship.

We were all hanging around the perimeter of the crowd, pretending to be interested in the bull that Benunni was spewing and checking out the young ladies. Benunni was dramatically explaining the use of the UDATS video system and was showing the tape of one of our underwater repair jobs and how we inspect a ship's hull.

"This is the screw of a nuclear cruiser. Each blade is approximately six feet long as you can see where the diver is pointing. The diver in this video just happens to be standing behind you. HT-3 Workman, please step forward and acknowledge yourself. A real hero, ladies and gentlemen."

Workman was in the spotlight and smiled, blushing from all the attention. Then he saw a cute girl giving him the eye and he focused on her, giving her his famous "I'm helpless" look that women fell for all the time. From the look of this girl, Workman was going to get lucky, real soon. The crowd's attention had been drawn away from watching the underwater repair video and Benunni started explaining the various pieces of diving equipment that we used.

"These are the Navy's old reliable Mark 5 diving helmets," he said, pointing to the helmets on either side of the aquarium. "These are used for salvage work and any diving job where the diver needs extra protection from the underwater elements."

"What do you mean by salvage work?" asked one of the women.

"Oh God, she picked up Benunni's cue. Here comes the tunneling story," I whispered to Workman, who nodded, rolling his eyes. We both had heard this story in many forms, several times, with many different people functioning as the hero. We both could almost mouth the story, word for word, along with Benunni. This is an informal rule that sailors follow: "If I've done the deed, or was merely there, then I'm the hero. If I heard about the deed, and nobody knows I wasn't there, then I did it and I'm the hero." In this case, we knew Benunni was full of shit because at diving school we'd heard this story several times by different instructors. Each instructor miraculously had been the hero of the same story. How could this be?

Benunni dramatically railed on. "We were trying to unbeach a ship that had gotten stuck in the mud in one of the river banks off the Mekong Delta in Vietnam. It was very intense because our Seal team had been attacked by Viet Cong at the same place two days before. We couldn't pull the ship off because the mud suction was too great. The only way we could loosen the ship up was to use the high pressure water hose to tunnel away the mud and create a bubble under the ship to break the suction. Well, I was the most experienced diver, so I donned the Mark 5 and proceeded to tunnel my way under the ship. As long as the water was blasting out, the tunnel stayed open. But if the water pressure was turn off or reduced, the mud would start to fill in the tunnel.

"Our unit came under attack and the water hose was hit, dropping the pressure in the hose. The mud started flowing in around me. I tried to make my way out of the tunnel before it filled in completely. I was dragging my hose with me and couldn't make it out in time. I was completely surrounded by mud and could barely move. Some of you might ask why I didn't drop the hose? Well, the reason is that it was my only way of getting out. Eventually the water pressure would be turned back on – that is hopefully turned back on – and you'd have to blast your way back out of the mud. At this point, the mud had me trapped under the ship. The guys up top told me what was happening but that didn't help my situation. All I could think of was I'm glad the Navy used this solid Mark 5 suits or I'd have been crushed."

While Benunni was adding more mud to his mud-tunneling escape story, the video monitor scene changed suddenly. There was Benunni's devilish face as he pointed to the beautiful Miss April on the poster. At first, only a few people noticed the screen, then more and more turned to see what was going on. Benunni was oblivious to this and continued with his escape story. There, on the screen, and clear as day, was Benunni, the macho diver, who was feeling and licking Miss April in front of the open house guests and the entire Ladies Auxiliary.

"Oh, my God," shrieked one of the older ladies.

Benunni, at first, thought she was commenting on how wonderful his mud escape story was. Then he realized that he had lost his audience and looked over at us for an explanation. With big smiles on our faces, Workman and I both pointed to the video screen. Benunni almost died on the spot. He was speechless for the first time in his life. His face turned bright red, his hands started opening and shutting, and you could tell he was looking frantically for the nearest exit. From the evil looks he was getting from the Ladies Club, running was probably the best thing he could do, and out the back door he ran.

I quickly stepped in and announced, "Well, ladies and gentlemen, that concludes the diving locker tour. I'm sure you'll never forget this.

If you'll follow me, I'll show you to the ship fitters shop, where they repair all sorts of really neat things." As the crowd hustled out quickly, that lucky, son-of-a-bitch Workman got the phone number of the girl who was giving him the eye.

Benunni, "the Italian Stallion", as we nicknamed him, was doing his best to hide out for the next two weeks before our cruise. We kept leaving messages on his locker. Benunni report to the Captains stateroom immediately. And the message would be signed with our division officer's name. Or whenever someone would open the door to the dive locker and Benunni was in the back room, we'd yell, "Attention on deck," which meant that the Captain had entered. Benunni would scurry out the back door as fast as he could and hide for about an hour. Whenever the Senior Chief would ask where he was, we'd just say he was out fucking off somewhere. Then Senior Chief would yell at him, when he'd finally get the nerve to sneak back in. God, it was nice having Benunni by the balls. And for two weeks we squeezed hard.

Chapter 7

BOHICA

Every Navy ship needs a good motto to motivate the personnel, as Captain Horner of the USS Puget Sound announced to his Executive Officer "It will give the crew extra pride, and will make the command look good."

To encourage the crew to come up with ideas for a motivational motto, Captain Horner offered one week basket, or free leave, at the port of choice. The Captain was right about motivating the crew on this. One week of free leave from the grind of 12-hour workdays, and standing watches on top of that, would be paradise. The crew was getting worn down from the exhausting work schedule. The motto suggestions poured in by the hundreds, and ran the gamut from terrible to perverse to really good. The department heads were the judges, and they would pick two selections from each of their perspective departments. Then, the Executive Officer would break it down to two choices, with Captain Horner making the final decision.

Many creative minds were at work. This, in itself, was the stuff from which trouble was made on board the ship. From this creative energy, a work of genius from Molder Second Class Don Madowsky was produced. As a molder, he made patterns and casts for metal repair parts for the ship's machinery. Most of his work was done alone. This gave him a lot of time to think about creating a fabulous motto, its historical explanation, and an illustration to go along with it.

As a high school student from the Pacific Northwest, Madowsky always had a fascination with Indian culture and history and loved to draw pictures of muscular Indian warriors in battle. This fascination caused him to develop the winning motto and drawing.

The Executive Officer called to everyone assembled on the fantail of the ship "Attention on Deck" and out came Captain Horner.

"At ease. I know all of you have been waiting to hear who the winner of the motto contest is. I must say I couldn't believe what creative people I have on board. The selection process was very difficult, but one motto stood heads above all the rest. And the winner is.....he paused for effect, ML2 Madowsky."

There were groans from the losers and some applause, but the most shocked person in the crowd was Don Madowsky. The Captain raised his hands and everyone quieted down. While unfurling a large copy of an Indian warrior that Madowsky had included with his motto, he continued,

"The new motto is 'BOHICA, May the spirit live on. Because our ship, the Puget Sound, was named for a location in the Pacific Northwest, I figured this theme is appropriate. I'm going tell you a little about our new motto. BOHICA was the battle cry of the Mahia Indian tribe from the Columbia River area of Washington State. During a time when their tribe was having many hardships, attacks from other tribes, and sickness, they kept their spirit of cohesiveness going by looking to their great chief BOHICA. He called upon them to have great courage and moved the tribe to a new homeland near Oregon, where they were able to pull through and prosper once again. The tribe went through many more hardships in their history. Every time they were faced with what seemed to be insurmountable obstacles, the spirit of BOHICA was called upon and they managed to find a way to get through. This is the spirit that I see in our crew today. When we have what seems to be an insurmountable work load, we always manage to get it done – much in the same spirit as the Mahia's BOHICA. Congratulations Petty Officer Madowsky and just don't have too much fun on your leave."

"Attention on deck," announced the Executive Officer.

"And may the spirit live on," the Captain shouted as he turned and walked away.

BOHICA fanaticism began. Department heads instructed everyone in their divisions to embrace and live with the spirit. BOHICA was everywhere. It was painted on bulkheads, molded into plaques, and added to the ship's stationery. The baseball team had the emblem on its uniforms and the Captain had a silk screen made and printed up 5000 T-shirts to bring the spirit into our lives after work hours as well. It was almost like the McCarthy-era Communist hunts of the '50s, because if you didn't profess your undying loyalty to the spirit of BOHICA you were branded an unbeliever, or worse, a blasphemous spirit killer. It got to the point where sailors were cutting paper feathers and wearing them on their hats.

A new language was even formed with money becoming wampum, alcohol was firewater, the hookers in the bars were squaws. If a sailor was a devout follower of the BOHICA motto, he was known as a Tonto. The standard greeting was no longer, "Good morning" or "Good afternoon," it was now, "How!" spoken with the hand raised and palm forward. A standard conversation was, "Hey, you going out tonight?" "Ya, I've got a little wampum, maybe throw down some firewaters and check out the squaws, if Chief Tonto lets us out early enough."

When the ship pulled into Palma de Majorca, Spain, Madowsky quickly took his one week basket leave and toured the whole beautiful island, having a great time. He was glad he was able to get the leave out of the way, because he was getting very nervous about the whole BOHICA thing.

It had been about two months into the BOHICA phenomenon when Madowsky stopped by the diving locker to drop off some molded solid brass diving helmets for diving plaques.

"How, Ski," I greeted him. He just smiled and handed over the brass helmets.

"Here they are. Got any coffee?"

"Ya, sit down and I'll squirt you a cup." Squirting coffee came from the sound the coffee maker made as it brewed the coffee, spewing or squirting out the liquid. The old malfunctioning coffee machine groaned and moaned, sounding like it was having a really good orgasm.

"Gee if I felt as good as that coffee maker sounds, I'd be a really happy guy," said Madowsky.

"You're looking pretty stressed there, Ski. What's up?"

"Well, they're going to find out sooner or later. I just hope it's after we get back."

"I hate to say it but I've been hearing some rumblings going around. All it takes is one Tonto to figure it out and the shit is really going to hit the fan. Well, at least you got your leave. It would have been a drag to have it there, only to be snatched away at the last minute."

Nelson, Workman, and West came in the locker and said their "Hows" to Ski with big smiles on their faces. They were all in the know about BOHICA and loving every deceptive minute of it.

"Hey, good job on these helmets, Ski," West said." At least you'll

be right at home making license plate molds after the Captain finds out."
Everyone laughed but Madowsky.

" Shit. What am I going to do?" whined Madowsky.

"I don't think it's going to happen for a while, anyway. Haven't
you heard of killing the messenger? Can you imagine the XO telling the
Captain what a fool he made out of himself?" I smiled at the thought.

Everyone present agreed that no one would be stupid enough to
inform Captain Horner of the joke that Madowsky had played on him.
For the next month, through the grapevine on the ship, more and more
people found out the true meaning of the spirit of BOHICA. Finally, one
night while the CO was sleeping, the Executive Officer called all the
officers to the wardroom for a top secret meeting.

"Men, I just got done talking to the CO of the USS Barney, who is
an academy buddy of mine, and he asked me why we were putting an
insulting message all over our ship. Do any of you know what BOHICA
really means?"

He looked around the room, but none of the officers looked up. None
of them wanted to show any sign that they knew what he was talking
about. Some officers even tried to feign innocent facial expressions. All
of them knew what was coming next.

"We're the laughing stock of the whole damn fleet. You know that?"
He shouted angrily. "Which one of you is going to tell the Captain that
BOHICA means –Bend Over, Here It Comes Again?– My God, we're
announcing to the fleet that we fuck our men in the ass and are proud of
it!"

No one answered. The room was silent. It was very hard for some
of the officers not to laugh, seeing the distress of the XO. His face was
the color of a ripe tomato with sweat beading up on his forehead. The
Executive Officer's career was on the line because of BOHICA. Even
though Captain Horner picked the winning motto from two choices,
shit always flowed downhill in the Navy, and he was the first one down
the hill – unless he quickly stepped aside, letting it hit an even lower
ranking officer.

For all the officers sitting in this secret meeting, there wasn't a thing
they could say or do to solve the crisis. In accordance with Navy protocol,
the only solution was to run for cover and to stay out of the way of
flowing shit. The Executive Officer decided that it was the responsibility

of Commander Matronelli, who had the unfortunate privilege of having Don Madowsky in his department. The other officers looked over at Matronelli with concern, but they were all relieved because the shit was now flowing away from them. Everyone was dismissed, and they all quickly left the wardroom. Matronelli remained, sitting stone-like.

Matronelli was obviously in mental anguish. It wasn't his fault, and as a professional military man, this incident should logically have no impact on his career. But on the other hand, common sense and rational thinking frequently had no place in the US Navy. As these conflicting thoughts must have struggled in his head, he went directly to the Repair Department berthing, angrily looking for Madowsky.

Unknown to all the officers who had gathered secretively in the wardroom, their meeting had not been as secret as they thought. The ship's phone in this room had a knob on it, and if left slightly off the hook, another phone, tuned to that number, could hear everything said in the wardroom. As soon as the officers started gathering, Seaman Apprentice Doon, who was doing his 90-day mess-cooking duty as wardroom orderly, set the phone on the ready position. The duty of phone setup had been passed down from mess cook to mess cook for years. No secret was ever safe if spoken in the wardroom. Also, the system could be set up as a party line in which several phones could listen in if the correct number sequence was dialed.

SA Doon, a wanna-be diver who would do anything to be on the good side of the divers, called the dive locker to alert all that something important was going on. I called Madowsky and the entire diving crew mustered in the diving locker. We set up the phone and quietly waited for the meeting to start. West took the speaker out of the mouthpiece so our noises could not be heard from the other side of the connection. We heard the whole meeting. Afterwards, Madowsky started to lose it.

"God, what am I going to do? I'm fucked."

Still in shock from actually getting the news he knew would be coming sooner or later, Madowsky flopped back in his chair with a desperate look on his face. I walked up with a big smile and poked Madowsky in the arm.

"Hey, what's the problem here? This is so easy. Remember who we're dealing with here – a bunch of tight-assed, load-sweating career officers. What are you going to do? Crawl in there licking his boots, asking for forgiveness? Shit, no!"

I was on a role like a Baptist preacher. "It's time for action. First, you told me there really was a, what the fuck was the tribe's name, the ma-jerk-offs or something?"

"Mahia's," Madowsky corrected.

"Mahia's, Ma-jerk-offs, whatever. You're an expert on these Indians. Right?" Madowsky still wasn't comprehending, and sulked in the chair.

"Right!" I shouted with great enthusiasm. Walking quickly around the diving locker, building the excitement. "Right!" I shouted at Madowsky again.

"Right!" Madowsky shouted back, still not getting it, but feeling the positive energy building, he was starting to get the spirit of my presentation.

"Now, they know absolutely nothing about BOHICA except what you put on that entry paper. We need an Academy Award performance out of you. You go in to Matronelli like there's nothing's wrong, and act totally innocent about the whole thing. What's he going to write you up for? That way, it's all on his shoulders. Can you imagine what he's going to be going through with no scapegoat and having to report back to the Executive Officer that there really is a BOHICA. It obviously has two meanings and you only knew the historical meaning. For the rest of the cruise, the officers will be shitting themselves every time they hear about the spirit of BOHICA."

Madowsky was absolutely beaming.

"Ya, Ya, Ya!" he yelled. Madowsky jumped up from his chair and with a huge smile on his face, walked to the door and reverently said, "May the spirit of BOHICA live on." We fell apart laughing after he left.

Madowsky wandered around the ship for about an hour before Matronelli found him.

"Come to my office, right now!" he ordered very sternly.

At a brisk pace, they went to the Repair Department Headquarters and entered Commander Matronelli's office.

"Close the door," Matronelli said angrily.

Madowsky did so and was about to sit down.

"No one gave you permission to sit!"

Madowsky was calm and collected, trying hard not to smile. He knew he had Matronelli by the balls.

"I'm on to you, you asshole, with your little BOHICA scam. You thought you were pretty smart, but now it's turned around and bit you in the ass."

Madowsky listened intently and with a very calm, serious look on his face said, "What are you talking about?"

"You know exactly what I'm talking about," he screamed, standing up and starting to lose control. His hands were squeezing the edge of his desk so hard that his knuckles were turning white and his jaw was clinched so tightly that it looked like his teeth would explode. He didn't expect Madowsky to be so calm or to give him the appearance of innocence. He expected him to crumble under his superior authority and confess the whole thing, begging for mercy. His mind was scrambling to come up with something new to yell at him. Either Madowsky was the best actor he'd ever seen, or he really didn't know anything about the scam. Sitting back down and calming himself a little, he continued, "You were the one who thought of the BOHICA motto? I mean, someone didn't give it to you to turn in for them?"

"No, I thought up the motto myself, and I'm proud that it was picked. I'm not sure what you mean by scam. The Mahia Indians and BOHICA are real. I grew up in the Pacific Northwest and even knew some Mahia Indians at my school," he lied. He was enjoying turning up the burners on his commander. Now, filled with more confidence, Madowsky said, "I don't appreciate you talking to me this way, and if there isn't anything else, I'll be on my way."

"You mean you didn't use BOHICA as a joke for 'Bend Over, Here It Comes Again'?" Matronelli said meekly.

"Well, I've heard that going around, but I think it was just made up after the motto was chosen. You know how sailors can be jealous of people who have more power or think of better ideas then they can." Madowsky knew that this fed right into Matronelli's short man's syndrome. Matronelli nodded in agreement to what Madowsky had said. "I'm sure you've run into that in your Navy career." He paused and added, "If there is nothing else, I have mid-watch tonight so I need to get some sleep," he lied again.

"Get out of here," Matronelli said, obviously depressed.

Walking out the door and into the passageway Madowsky was ready to burst, but he had to make it back to the diving locker before he could get out of character. It was the longest walk he'd ever taken. He wanted no one outside the diving locker to know the charade he'd pulled. If word got out, rumors would spread like wild fire and he'd be canned for sure.

Finally Madowsky made it back to the aft part of the ship where the diving locker was located. He spent the next few minutes in splendid glory, relating word for word, everything that went on, encouraged to exaggerate even more by the supportive laughter.

Back at the Repair Department Office, Matronelli was stuck between a rock and a hard place. Either Madowsky lied and tricked him, or what he said about BOHICA was true. Either way, he was screwed. Madowsky seemed to have all the answers. How could he have known what he was going to accuse him of?

"Madowsky Must have been telling the truth," whined Matronelli to himself. "God, I'm not going to get any sleep tonight. What am I going to tell the XO?"

Everyone knew that Matronelli was going to take the heat for the Captain's unfortunate motto selection. And everyone also knew that soon the Commander would not only represent, but would personally embody, the true spirit of BOHICA – that Matronelli would soon uphold true Navy tradition and bend over, because here it comes again.

Chapter 8

Pumping The Loaf

My morning ritual was to get up at 4:30 a.m. and stop by the bake shop, located next to the galley, to see Mess Specialist Third Class Roger "Pillsbury Dough Boy" Bostic. He was the best baker in the world, next to my own mother. Bostic did nothing but bake. His sole purpose on the ship was to make fresh bread each morning for Captain Horner's breakfast.

Because Bostic was such a good baker, he got out of all the crummy stuff that mess cooks have to do, like midnight rations cooking, which was serving leftovers to the guys going on and coming off the midnight watches. He didn't have to line cook, do stocking, or supply requisitions. He was in his own little baking kingdom from midnight until 9a.m. Besides making the captain's bread, he made wonderful cinnamon rolls, flaky croissants, donuts and Danish pastries that made the whole crew show up early for breakfast.

Every morning I stopped by to evaluate the baked goods, to see if they were of high enough quality to serve the rest of the crew. Everyone wanted to get freebies from MS3 Bostic, but only a select few were allowed inside the inner domain of the baker's castle to test his products.

When Bostic was new on the ship, he stopped by the dive boat to see us working, and asked me some questions. As the conversation went, the subject of knives came up. Everyone wanted a Diver's K-Bar combat knife. It was a solid one-piece, straight steel fighting knife with a leather handle that could only be acquired by the Navy's special warfare units which included Seals, Explosive Ordinance Disposal Divers, and Deep Sea Divers.

Bostic loved knives and had a collection of over 300 from around the world, but he didn't have a K-Bar. The divers always kept boxes of these knives in the diving locker because they could be traded for almost anything. If you couldn't get something done in a timely manner, you could barter with a K-Bar to get anything. I did not miss my opportunity to get in good with the new baker, so I gave him a K-Bar later that day. That sealed our friendship.

I stuck my head into the bake shop door and yelled, "Hey, Doughy, you up to standards today?"

"You wouldn't be here if I wasn't, yeast sniffer."

"Yeast sniffer? I heard that bakers can't get it to rise unless they sprinkle yeast on it. That's why all their girl friends have yeast infections," I joked with him.

"You're downright gross, Fredrickson. See if this will shut you up," as he handed me a fresh, warm cinnamon roll.

"This roll is looking pretty small, or are you just teasing me today?" I said as I took a bite.

"Gee, isn't that what your girl friend said to you the other night?" Bostic jabbed back at me. It went on like this, day after day.

"I always notice that we have brown bread when the bakery looks the cleanest," I commented one morning. Or, another day I'd ask, "Is that a croissant or an oversized sculpture of your dick?" And, if I really wanted to work him, I'd ask, "Why are you always smiling when the Danish has the creamiest center?"

Banter went on every morning and the hardest part for me was trying to figure out a new corny baker's joke each day. But one morning, Bostic was a changed person. He wasn't his normal cheerful self. Instead, he was throwing things around and yelled at me, "No freebies today, asshole. Get out of here."

I stood there wondering what possibly could have upset Bostic.

"Get out or I'll throw your ass out of here."

I walked in very calmly and concerned "First thing you're gonna do is sit your ass down and tell me what's bothering you. I've never seen you like this before."

Bostic's shoulders slumped down and he slowly walked over to a flour drum and sat.

"She's leaving me," Bostic confided softly.

"Who?" I asked.

"My wife, Peggy."

Then, Roger Bostic told me his story. He was born and raised in the mountains of West Virginia. His father died when he was very young, so he was raised by his mother. He wasn't what you'd call a handsome guy.

At 13 years old, he was 6–3" and skinny as a rail. He was nicknamed Icabod because he resembled Icabod Crane in the Legend of Sleepy Hollow. The name stuck with him all through high school. He never had a date or anything resembling a relationship. So, Roger spent a lot of time working with his mom in the kitchen. She was the closest thing to a mountain caterer that you could get. Weddings, funerals, graduations or any other reason to celebrate or have people come together, Roger's mom did the baking. Her pies, bread, and buttermilk biscuits were legendary around the whole community. It was considered an insult to the attendees of a function if the host didn't have some of Roger's mom's creations.

After high school, Roger continued to help his mom in the baking business until one day she had a heart attack and died. He was 20 years old and his skills were hunting and cooking. He knew he didn't want to spend the rest of his life in the West Virginia mountains, so he joined the Navy to see the world.

Roger met Peggy in San Diego when he was going to Mess Specialist "A" school. It was love at first sight because Peggy was the first girl who liked him. They were married two months later, the day after Roger graduated from Mess school. He was immediately stationed on the USS Puget Sound out of Norfolk, Virginia, and within 30 days of arrival there, left on a six month Mediterranean cruise.

Peggy was another story though. Her family was always on the move. Her father was a small-time con artist and her mother spent a lot of time in bars. She and her little brother had to fend for themselves on many occasions. Their relatives were used for a place to sleep, eat, and, "to sponge as much as you can from" as her mom would say. So when Peggy and her brother showed up at their doors, the welcome wasn't a happy one.

At 16, Peggy was on her own. She would hop from one guy to another, living where she could, and taking everything she could from each relationship before moving on. While in San Diego, she met Roger and immediately knew she had a big fish to be reeled in. She easily manipulated Roger into falling in love with her, then into marrying her. The thought of nice, clean Navy housing and a steady income was too good to pass up.

They moved into a small two-bedroom military housing unit and three weeks later Roger was off to sea for six months. The majority of Roger's paycheck was allotted to a joint bank account. That way, "we could start a little savings for vacation or a family, when you get back," Peggy told him.

It was obvious to me that Roger had been worked real hard. But I couldn't say anything about it, in Roger's current state. So, I went the Navy way and told Roger that he had to try and fix things up.

"First, you need to ask for emergency leave. So, put in a request chit and get things started there. Don't tell her you're coming home. You want to surprise her. That way you'll get a better idea of what really is going on."

Roger calmed down and hung his head. He was on the verge of crying now with all his pent-up emotions. "I guess you're right. I'm sorry for yelling at you. You're the only real friend I've got on this tub. Thanks for listening," he said.

"I'll go and get you a chit right now. Oh, by the way, there is a two cinnamon roll fee for psychological counseling," I added.

That got a smile from Roger "Here, take three. You're worth it."

Things seemed to calm down a bit because Roger got approval from his division officer and department head to go on emergency leave. But that's where it ended. Captain Horner disapproved the chit saying, "We don't have enough manpower to cover his absence."

What the Captain really meant was that he didn't want to miss Bostic's daily bread and pastries, his favorite thing in the world. The Captain was heard to say frequently that Bostic's fantastic bakery goods were the best reason to get up in the morning. The Captain also knew that the odds of MS3 Bostic going AWOL were very high. Sailors with marital problems most often didn't come back, and the Captain wasn't going to take the chance of losing his baker.

When his emergency leave was denied, Bostic went ballistic for one day. Then he seemed to calm down suddenly. Every once in awhile he would blurt out, "Fuck the Navy, Fuck Captain Horner," and that would be it. And once in awhile he would walk around with a funny grin on his face and when we asked what he was thinking about, he would say, "Oh, I'm just thinking about fucking over Captain Horner," and he would smile and walk away.

There was another character on the ship who would soon enter

Bostic's life - Ernesto Lubag. He was the Filipino Joe Friday of the Master-at-Arms Squad. As a 1st-class machinist mate, he was a failure. When everybody else was making chief, he kept failing his test.

Lubag was getting desperate for some recognition that would put him over the top with the selection board for chief. He was temporarily assigned to Master-at-Arms duty. As a First Class Petty Officer this was his last enlistment before he would be forced to retire, and he was looking for positive recognition that would help him make chief.

Now most of the people who were assigned to the Master-at-Arms were sailors who were either incompetent or couldn't get along in their divisions. MM1 Lubag was both. When his division chief had a chance to dump him on the MAA, it took him two seconds to write Lubag's name on the transfer sheet.

MM1 Lubag was known as Deputy Dog. He would stay up all hours of the night sneaking and sniffing around the ship trying to catch people not standing their watches properly, or his ultimate hard-on was to catch someone smoking dope.

Some of the guys used to sneak up on him when he was on the prowl and jump out, scaring the hell out of him. After he would gain his composure, he'd say in his thick accent, "God dom it! I go to wite you up fo disrespect a Superior Petty Officer." He'd then stalk off, thinking he'd intimidated the offending sailor. As he went down the passageway, "Deputy Dog always gets his man", echoed after him.

One problem was that Deputy Dog couldn't speak, read, or write English very well. He'd taken the chief's test 10 times and failed miserably when all it took to pass was spelling his name correctly. He also had another secret that he didn't want anyone to know. When he took the English test to qualify for the US Navy years ago, his younger brother took the test for him. His younger brother was now a Master Chief E-9, and he was still an E-6 1st Class Petty Officer, which was very embarrassing to Deputy Dog.

When he first enlisted, Deputy Dog chose to be a machinist mate because it was easy to make higher ratings here. Who in their right mind would want to work in a 120 - 130-degree engine room all day, week after week, year after year? It wasn't a job, it was a sentence. They didn't call it the hole for nothing. As a machinist mate, Deputy Dog wasn't very mechanically inclined at all. He was raised in the rural provinces of the Philippines where he would skin a monkey for barbecue or prepare a tasty dog for a holiday dinner, but measuring valve clearances or making tuning adjustments to the main engines were really hard for him to understand. Even the Chief tried to teach him in a way that never failed to get anyone else to understand: sex.

"Now Lubag, the piston is like a penis and the cylinder is like a pussy. The piston goes in, the piston goes out, and if it isn't lubricated it burns up." This explanation didn't help him understand engines any better, but Deputy Dog admitted that it did help to explain why his penis hurt after sex with his wife.

After 26 years in the Navy, Deputy Dog figured the only way he was going to make chief was if he busted enough guys. The higher-ups would then think more highly of him. But, after attempting to read his offense report chits with improper grammar, misspelled words, and poor sentence structure, over three quarters of his report chits were thrown away because he had not explained well enough what the offending person had done wrong. He wrote the way he spoke.

REPORT CHIT
Article: Improper Watch Stan
Narrative: Proper watch stan not stood. Soda Drink Stan on watch. No look roun He do nothing. Bad watch stan.

None of the other MAAs would help him with his reports and the MAA Chief would tell him, "Do it again until it's right. How the hell else are you going to learn to write English?" Behind his back, they all laughed and mimicked his reports:

Man on report, Ahhhhh won't stop sleep Ahhhhh, say fuck you Deputy Dog Ahhhhh vedy much disrespect, say go stan watch youself ass hoe Ahhhh, I'm short, my dick small an I going to get back at tall, big dick sailors, Ahhhhh.

Instead of his superiors thinking more highly of him, Deputy Dog became the butt of every small dick and short joke that could be cracked. It was Deputy Dog's worst nightmare when the Randy Newman song, "Short People" hit the charts. Everywhere he went, guys would hum or sing the song with improvised lyrics. "Short people have no reason to live," echoed through the passageways as Deputy Dog walked by.

Benunni also now worked in the MAA's office with Deputy Dog. One of his favorite things was to send Deputy Dog on secret missions: "I've heard scuttlebutt about dopers" or "They've been sleeping on watch" or "Rumor has it that gambling is going on." One time he had Deputy Dog hide for four hours in the CHT pump room, the collecting and holding tank room for the ship's sewage. Benunni claimed to have heard that's where the dopers go to smoke out.

Benunni alerted us in the dive locker of Deputy Dog's pending arrival and with the help of my Hull Technician buddies, we left open one of the gas testing valves on the tank so it would emit a noxious smell. We also turned off the exhaust fan. The room smelled terrible, like a damp cesspool. With Deputy Dog hiding out in this dark, smelly place, Benunni would send someone down to the seventh deck every 20 minutes or so to keep Deputy Dog awake and alert. This messenger entered and opened and closed the door whispering, "Have you got the stash?" or some other drug-related phrase. The secret messenger would leave before Deputy Dog could sneak out of his hiding place under the 2000-gallon tank, and see who it was. Deputy Dog stayed under the tank for four hours, but after a while, he couldn't stand the smell anymore, became nauseous, and had to leave. On his way up, he passed through the engineering berthing space where everyone knew what was going on.

"Hey, Deputy Dog, you smell like shit. What have you been doing swimming in the shit tank?"

He ignored that one.

"Hey, Deputy Dog what are those brown stains on your knees?"

After looking down at his pants and seeing the sailor smiling at him, "Fuck you ass hoe," and stormed up the ladder. .

The ironic part was that the CHT room was where the dopers actually went to smoke out because it was the only compartment that had a strong exhaust fan. There were only two keys to the room and they were controlled by people on the inside. The room was left open to pull this trick, thus eliminating it from Deputy Dog's future list of places to search each night on his nightly prowls.

The next night, Deputy Dog was on his typical midnight prowl, cruising around with his flashlight and black nightstick. He was the only MAA to carry a nightstick. This phallic symbol of power brought on a whole new series of jokes for him to endure.

"Hey, Deputy Dog, is that wishful thinking in your hand or are you just trying to be one of the brothers? Long, black, and hard?"

"Hey, Deputy Dog, that's a nice sitting stool you have there."

Deputy Dog replied, "What you mean?"

"With that brown stain on the end of it, I figured you sat on it a lot."

Deputy Dog looked at the stick, then figured out what the person meant and said his standard, "Fuck, you ass hoe," and quickly walked away, laughter following him.

He stopped threatening to put people on report because everyone knew that he would have to fill out the "dreaded report chit" and be the butt of more broken English jokes.

Deputy Dog liked to go by the bakery because it smelled so good. He never got any handouts but the smell drew him like a magnet. Walking toward the door of the bakery, Deputy Dog sniffed the wonderful aromas. He heard someone inside speaking in a very hostile, mean voice. The door to the bakery was one of those half doors that was split with a top and bottom half. He bent over and tried to look through the crack between the two parts of the door. He was just barely able to see someone in there, and the words were clearer now.

"Fuck Captain Horner, Fuck the Navy. Fuck Captain Horner, Fuck the Navy. Fuck Captain Horner, Fuck the Navy," repeated over and over and faster and faster.

Deputy Dog slowly opened the bottom half of the door and bent over to go through. Very quietly he crept up on the unsuspecting person who was cursing the esteemed ship's captain. The idea of catching someone doing something wrong was thrilling. He finally came to the bulkhead where the person was saying faster and with more anger, "Fuck Captain Horner, Fuck the Navy."

Deputy Dog took a peak around the corner and was shocked speechless at what he saw. MS3 Roger Bostic was standing with his pants unzipped and a fully erect penis that was jammed into the center of a loaf of bread dough. He was pumping the loaf back and forth on his erected member as he spoke. Bostic suddenly got a happy look on his face and let out a loud, ah-h-h-h-h, releasing his anger and hatred of the Navy and Captain Horner into the Captain's favorite loaf of breakfast bread. Bostic smiled and turned to see Deputy Dog staring at him, the loaf was still impaled on his cock. They both just stared at each other not moving.

Finally, Deputy Dog screamed, "You on report, Homo-man!" and ran from the bakery to get witnesses. On his way through the half door, he forgot to duck low enough and hit his head on the bottom edge, nearly knocking himself out. Looking back and seeing Bostic standing there with the loaf still on his cock, he frantically crawled out the door. Halfway down the passageway, he jumped up and rocketed to the MAA's office.

After Bostic had tried to get emergency leave for three months, it took less then 24 hours to process him out of the Navy. It was probably the fastest Captain's Mast in Naval history. Bostic was reduced in rank to E-1 and given a General Discharge with less than Honorable Disposition.

The Captain gave Deputy Dog two days basket or free leave and a Letter of Accommodation for his outstanding detective work. Deputy Dog strutted around the ship acting like he'd really done something important. He boasted that because of him, the Navy, America, and even the world were now a better place to live.

Everyone who knew Bostic felt bad for him, because they understood why he did what he did. No one ever heard from him again.

Benunni came down to the diving locker, chuckling away.

"What's so funny, no-load?" asked West.

Benunni's new nick name was "no-load" since he'd transferred to the MAA's office. Benunni would brag, "Life's easy. All I do is bust stupid motherfuckers. And if you guys fuck up, I'll bust your asses, too," and he'd smile and look around in a superior way. He thought he was really cool.

"Suggestion box is at an all time high since Homo-man got busted," he laughed.

Deputy Dog couldn't remember Bostic's name for the report and in his excitement, all he could call him was Homo-man. The name and the story went around the ship like wildfire. We figured that for three months, the Captain had been eating Bostic's special bread. The suggestion box to the Captain was loaded with well meaning advice and suggestions, all containing someone's name other then the real author's. Here are some of the suggestions for Captain Horner:

- Pumping the loaf should be the Navy's new fitness plan.
- Why can't the crew have the bread with the creamy center?
- Now the age-old question of how bread rises has been answered.
- Homo-man wasn't doing anything perverted: he was just using the Navy's new condom.
- The Captain has the whitest teeth we've ever cum across.
- Bostic was just following the Navy's new safe sex program.
- Wear a loaf to be protected from STDs (Sexually Transmitted Diseases).
- Bostic, Bostic he's our man, Cum in a loaf as fast as you can,
- Captain, Captain knew his trick, He gave that loaf a great big lick.

The suggestion box was continually crammed with creative expressions. This event produced as much participation as the BOHICA Motto Contest some months ago. "Homo-man was here" or "Homo-man strikes again" was written all over the ship. This phrase was accompanied by an illustration of an erect penis with a loaf of bread stuck on it. But, always next to the phrase and illustration was something white smeared on it. The logo appeared even in very bold places like outside the passageway in front of the Captain's stateroom. There was even a rumor of a Homo-man secret society with the whole purpose to keep Bostic's legend alive. Rumors were the most fun and the divers were in the thick of it.

After a couple of weeks of Homo-man hysteria and commotion, the joke died down. Captain Horner had been profoundly embarrassed at first, but was starting to get his arrogant self back. One of his personal attendants who cleaned up his stateroom, passed around the story that when the Captain walked into his stateroom bathroom one day, on the wall by his mirror was a long glob of a white, substance running down the wall. Written next to it, in large bold letters was, Homo-man strikes again!

Chapter 9

Mike "Sea Hunt" Nelson, The Space Cadet

Mike Sea Hunt Nelson made it through dive school by the skin of his teeth. He failed his initial tests in diving physics and medicine and had to go through remedial study, or stupid study, as it was known. He eventually passed both of these sections with a 75 percent, which is the lowest score you can have and still pass. While in the third hell week SCUBA pool phase, he lucked out because his partner was a SEAL who wouldn't let him quit. The SEAL got in Sea Hunt's face and would scream, threaten, and literally carried him through the pool confidence building part of the school.

"Don't think, just do what I say! I've never lost a buddy and you're not going to be the first," his SEAL partner would yell. And like a mindless robot, Sea Hunt would do what he was told, no matter how hard it was, mostly because he was scared shitless of his partner who had completed two tours in Vietnam on SEAL teams. Sea Hunt graduated last in his class.

When Sea Hunt checked on board the Puget Sound, we expected an inexperienced diver because he was newly graduated from diving school. But with the given name of Mike Nelson, the diving hero of the 60's TV show Sea Hunt starring Lloyd Bridges, we attributed far superior abilities to him than we should have. I immediately gave him his nickname.

Unfortunately, we expected too much from Sea Hunt. We thought he'd learn our procedures very quickly but we were dead wrong. On Sea Hunt's first working dive, he went down with me on a standard hull inspection of a destroyer in about two to four feet of visibility. He was very nervous before we went down, which is a bad sign because this was a really easy dive assignment. Conditions were good, with sunny, calm seas and no wind. When we hit the water and went through our regular equipment checks, I signaled Senior Chief that we were ready to go down. He gave us the okay. At first, I thought I was being attacked by an octopus because Sea Hunt was clamped onto me like an abalone to a rock. I finally pushed him off and handed him my hose so he wouldn't get lost from me. I needed some room to work.

I went through all the different checks with him, showing how to inspect the two main shafts and struts which held the shaft in place. Then we covered the rudders and the propeller. I showed him how to find a mark on the dunce cap on the end of the screw by locating the set screw on it and then moving clockwise until coming back to the screw again, marking each screw blade to not lose track of the blade number. That way if some damage was recorded or one had to return to it again later, the number could be easily found. I slowly went through each step for him, assuming that something was sticking. I checked everything off on my Plexiglas board with my grease pencil. Satisfied that we had covered all the different sections we needed to inspect, I signaled topside and we proceeded to the surface.

The Senior Chief and I went over the results and compared them with the last inspection to see if there were any changes. We always tried to have the same diver do the same ship because everyone had a slightly different way of measuring things, and this kept the results more consistent.

Now it was Sea Hunt's turn to try an inspection on his own. He looked like we were sending him on a suicide mission. His hands shook as we attached the nylon string to his wrist that was tied to the Plexiglas check-off list. Almost all tools were tied to the diver because it was easy to drop things while working. If tools were dropped, they disappeared in the slime and sludge that covered most of the harbor bottom. Losing any tools meant buying the dive locker a round of beers.

We hatted Sea Hunt with the MK 1 diving helmet which had full communication in it. This was much safer then the Jack Brown mask, which had only a side valve and no direct oral communication with topside. Senior Chief didn't want to risk putting Sea Hunt down on his first solo without communication. He quickly saw from Sea Hunt's emotional response that he wasn't going to be worth a shit on this cruise. Senior Chief had a very good instinct about what his guys were capable of, and he immediately saw Sea Hunt as a liability.

Senior Chief went over the dive plan with Sea Hunt and then sent him over the side. After going over his topside checks, he signaled okay to the Senior Chief and, with eyes as big as saucers, went down. Sea

Hunt came up again about 15 seconds later, far off to the right of the ship. Sometimes in low visibility it's easy to lose your direction, but in this case all Sea Hunt had to do was drop straight down and he'd land on the screw he was to inspect. We directed him over to the ship again and sent him down. Again, in about 15 seconds, he surfaced again saying he couldn't find the screw. By this time, we were all giving each other the "this guy 's really sad" look. We were hoping this was just first-dive jitters.

Again we directed him back to the stern of the ship and sent him down. Finally he made it to the screw and started his first hull inspection. We could hear the narrative of his work and everything seemed to be going okay. He came up after about 10 minutes and we looked at his results to compare them with my previous measurements. The first thing that jumped out at us was the fact that the screw that he had drawn on the Plexiglas board only had three blades on it. We questioned this because it couldn't be correct.

"There were only three blades on it," he said.

"On any Navy ship, the screws have either four or five blades. Only small boats have three blades," explained Senior Chief to Sea Hunt, totally exasperated. "Get back down there and get it right this time!"

Sea Hunt was hatted again and eventually found the screw. We know he didn't find it right away because his bubbles were coming up to the surface in all different places. In about five minutes, he came up and Senior Chief wouldn't let him climb up on the boat, insisting that he hand up the Plexiglas board so he could see his results. And there on the board was a picture drawn of a screw with five blades. The only problem was, this ship's screw only had four.

Senior Chief looked down at Sea Hunt and said, "Are you sure there are five blades on that screw?" Sea Hunt shook his head affirmatively. "Are you willing to bet 20 dollars on that?" He challenged. Sea Hunt shook his head negatively. "Then go back down and get it right this time."

Again after another circle swim to find the screw, he found it, drew another illustration and was back up again. Senior Chief yelled down at him, "How many?" Sea Hunt looked up with a face of a man who didn't have a clue. He held up four fingers, nervously.

West looking over the side yelled down, "God damn it Sea Hunt, you fucking idiot, there's five blades on that fucking screw. Now go back down and find five blades and don't come back up until you do."

As soon as Sea Hunt went back down again, everyone started laughing until the reality of the entire circumstance began to hit us. If Sea Hunt sucked that bad, then we were going to have to take up the slack, which meant diving a lot more. On cruises, we are in the water, seven days a week, 12 hours or more a day from 7 a.m. to sometimes late at night. The thought of having to dive more because of a weak link in the chain suddenly depressed us all. After about 10 minutes, Sea Hunt came up and Senior Chief signaled him to climb on board. When he came on deck, Senior Chief asked again, "How many?"

"I went over and over it again and I could only find four."

"Good, it's about fucking time. Now where's the inspection board?"

Sea Hunt looked around like he was trying to locate it and then did what turned out to be his patented move: With both hands he patted himself down from chest to legs and looked up astonished and said, "I think I dropped it."

How someone could drop a piece of equipment that was tied to your wrist was beyond us, but Sea Hunt had done it. At least we were going to get a beer out of it because if you lost a tool you bought the locker a round of beers. This was Sea Hunt's beginning, and unfortunately for us, his diving expertise didn't get any better.

Our main dilemma was that after a period of time, we all grew to like the guy personally, despite all his diving faults. He was a great guy to hang out with and topside he worked real hard. As long as he didn't go in the water, we liked having him around. Sea Hunt knew his diving skills sucked and he tried to take on more duties on the boat to make up for having us do more diving. It worked out okay. We had a silent system. I'd hate to think what might have happened to Sea Hunt if he turned out to be a jerk on top of it all. He became a part of our dive team and we all looked out for one another. Sea Hunt bought an awful lot of beer that year.

Chapter 10

Liberty In Naples

Naples, Italy, was a mixture of some of the most fascinating, beautiful and historical sights – as well as some of the most bazaar and depressing ones too. Pompeii, Herculaneum, the Isles of Capri, and Ithaca were fabulous historical sights, and at the opposite end of the spectrum were the street kids begging for money, the crumbling buildings and the slimy alleys, filled with overaged whores still trying to look young with thick, caked-on make-up. It made these aged streetwalkers look more like grotesque clowns as they attempted to seduce prospective customers.

Our first stop after getting off the liberty boat at fleet landing in Naples was the Seamans Bar on the second floor of a rickety building, across the street from the harbor. The Seamans Bar was a nice place, for Naples. Good, cheap food and drink, and no whores to bother you. It was either the first stop on the way in to the scum bar district, or the last stop, before catching the liberty boat at fleet landing to slam down a few coffees, to sober up before going back to the ship.

A group of divers was sitting out on the balcony of the Seamans Bar, which included Tim Workman, Mike "Sea Hunt" Nelson, "I quit partying" Jerry West, and BOHICA Madowsky. We all waited for the ice-cold Peroni beers to be delivered.

I looked down to street level and saw a very small Fiat pull up and park by the fountain across the street. Inside was a young couple who immediately starting to kiss and carry on.

"Hey, look at those two going at it," I said.

"I'll bet he's getting a little stiffy," Workman piped in.

"Hey, you know what they call an Italian with his cock in a pussy?" I said.

No one knew but there was a groan from everyone, because they were going to find out. They loved my jokes. They just wouldn't admit it.

"A Vienna sausage in a can. You know why?" Another groan. "Because it takes six of them little buggers to fill the hole in the can."

It was my joke, so I laughed the hardest. And then the retorts started.

"So, you're Eye-talian, eh Dan?" West began in a terrible Italian accent. "No wonder his locker's full of Vienna sausages. He just can't get enough of that Eye-talian meat."

"California Dan would know about Eye-talian cocks. Just ask any ricioni standing by the castle." Nelson continued.

Ricionis were drag queen whores that hung around an old castle that everyone had to pass by on their way to the whore bar area of town. Many of these ricionis were extremely good looking, and if you didn't know they were men, look out. In the dark, after a few beers, it's tough to tell until it's too late. Not that I would know or anything; that's just what I was told. But they all hung around the castle, so if you made it through that area, you were safe.

I remember one time when the aircraft carrier Enterprise and its battle group were in port. This landing produced 6,000 pussy-hungry, party animals in about a four-block area. The Naples bar zone was packed. I noticed two sailors talking to one of the ricionis. I quickly called one of them over and said,"Hey, man, that's a guy your friend's talking to."

He was half drunk. "No way, she's hot."

His friend walked off with the ricioni.

"Look I'm stationed here, and I'm telling you – that is a guy."

"No way!" He looked again in the direction of his friend, then back at me.

I put my hands, palm up and shrugged. "Hey, I'm just trying to help. If you don't want to listen, good luck."

Later that night I ran into this same guy again among the crowd.

"Wo-o-o man, you were right. When my friend came back, he didn't say a word and looked really freaked out. I put two and two together. I asked how big was his cock? Man, he almost died right there. He accused me of setting him up, and made me promise not to tell anyone." The sailor was laughing so hard he could barely stand up.

Now, back to the young couple parked in the car. After about 10 minutes of heavy touchy-feely, they pulled out a newspaper and started taping it to the car's windows. We watched with fascination. In a few minutes, they had covered all the windows and soon the car started rocking back and forth.

After watching for a while, an idea flashed in my mind. With a big smile, I conveyed the plan to the guys. They thought it was a stroke of genius. We all ran down the stairs, across the street and surrounded the car. We each grabbed the bumper of the tiny Fiat and started to shake the hell out of it. We started bouncing it up and down. We bounced it so hard, that the car came off the ground. Then, we picked up the Fiat and carried it on the sidewalk, next to the fountain, and ran back to the bar as fast as we could. We arrived back in our balcony seats to cheers and clapping of all the other patrons of the Seamans Bar who were watching us.

For a few minutes, nothing happened. The car was still. Then a finger scratched a small hole in the newspaper and an eyeball appeared and looked around. As fast as they could, they ripped off all the paper from the windows and started the car. They then realized they were on a high-curbed sidewalk. In sheer panic, the young man rammed into first gear and flew off with sparks flying as the car scraped the edge of the curb and bounced into the street.

"I'll bet that guy's wiener dropped as fast as that car off that curb," someone yelled out.

"We just did a service for the Catholic church. Birth control by fear. The Pope would be proud of us," I said

We had several rounds of beer bought for us and the divers had another story that would be blown out of proportion and spread on board the ship. It was a great way to start the evening.

This particular night, we'd been out until almost 2 a.m. and now had the daunting task of finding our way back to fleet landing. Lucky for us we had a landmark to give us directions. In the full moon, we saw Mt. Vesuvius, the famous volcano that covered the city of Pompeii with ashes and killed the entire population in less than 15 minutes. On the other side of Pompeii was the city of Medina which didn't fair much better, when lava lifted the entire city and carried it into the Mediterranean Sea, killing most of its population too. With the volcano to our backs, we knew we were going in the right direction.

Sea Hunt Nelson kept singing loudly his favorite Steve Miller song, "The Joker," except he changed the lyrics from, "They call me the joker" to "They call me the fucker, cause I keep fucking all night long," and many other inventive lines. We were having a hard time keeping Sea Hunt in line. The rule at fleet landing was that if you couldn't walk on the liberty boat back to the ship on your own power, you got put on report for drunk and disorderly. It was really strange because Nelson would get hammered so fast and stay wasted all night long and not remember most of the events the next day. He was harmless and never got in fights but it was as if he had some chemical imbalance. After only a few drinks, he would begin to act truly bizarre.

We decided that a trip to the Seamans Bar was in order to try and sober up Sea Hunt before we hit fleet landing to wait for the liberty boat to take us back to the ship. We ordered Sea Hunt two coffees. He slammed both of them down in seconds. We waited about 15 minutes until the coffee started taking effect and then continued on our way to fleet landing.

Everything was fine until we boarded the liberty boat. Sea Hunt, who had been pretty quiet for the last few minutes, seemed to feel the caffeine burst from the coffee and started singing his Joker song again with great exuberance. This time the words were changed to "They call me the fucker, cause I fuck the Navy in the ass."

"Shut that asshole up or or he goes on report when we hit the brow," the Chief of the boat yelled down.

We did our best to distract Sea Hunt by reminding him of the events of the night, which had been pretty fun. Remember the Hawaii bar? It's really weird because almost every country we visited had a Hawaii bar. They were all the same – fake palm trees and pictures of hula dancers painted on the walls, the same hookers who played the same games. One was the "I don't speak much English" game. So to combat this, we spoke our own special language. Tonight happened to be "tit" night. At the end of any given word, tit was added. Other times we used "O", "ski" or "y". A typical conversation could be Hey, Sea-tit Hunt-tit, get-tit me-tit a-tit beer-tit. Okay-tit? Or No-tit problem-tit, Dan-tit. Or I-tit want-tit one-tit for-tit Sea-tit Hunt-tit too-tit.

The whores at our table tried to figure out what we were saying. They pretended not to care, but after a while they got frustrated and asked, "What language are you guys speaking?" "Oh, we're speaking American titty slang. Would you like to learn some?" I asked in standard English.

One whore shook her head yes.

I got up behind her and put my hands on her breasts and started to count. With each count I squeezed one of her breasts and swung my butt from side to side with the count. "One-titty, two-titty, three-titty, four-titty, I'd like to teach you a little titty more." We were all laughing on the boat thinking about how flustered the whore got.

When the boat pulled up to the steps that went to the quarterdeck, Nelson had calmed down and was going through the motions of rolling the dice at the quarterdeck to see if he got searched or not. In every foreign port, to stem the flow of contraband entering the ship, the watch on the quarterdeck had a cup with a dice in it. Each night, one or two numbers were picked, and if your number was rolled, you were strip searched. Nelson's number came up.

Unfortunately for the watch, whenever Nelson drank Peroni beer, he got the Benunni fart syndrome. Nelson was escorted into the head to be searched. The first thing we heard was Nelson starting to sing his Joker song again, vilifying the Captain, the ship, and the Navy. Then a few seconds later the watch came out with a sickened look on his face.

"What's the problem?" the Chief asked him.

"The son of a bitch farted in there."

"Don't be a wimp. Go in there and finish the search."

"You go in there if you think it's safe, Chief."

The Chief went in and came out in less then 10 seconds with an equally sick look on his face. From outside the door, the Chief yelled in, "Goddamit, clean yourself up and get the fuck out of here, you asshole." He made sure that he wasn't near the air flow of the door.

Nelson had been told to strip down to his underwear, but seeing that divers rarely wear underwear, he got naked instead. When the Chief came in, Nelson had tried to fart so hard that he Hershey squirted himself, another Peroni syndrome. This filled the room with an even more wondrous odor. When Nelson realized what he had done to himself, he screamed out one of his mad doctor laughs.

When the Chief came back in, Nelson yelled loudly, "I'm ready for my body cavity search." He bent over and spread his butt cheeks, exposing his crapfilled butt hole.

In the few seconds that the chief was in there, his stomach nearly came out his mouth. As a result, searches were suspended for about 10 minutes, until the odor had cleared.

Now back on board, we had trouble getting Nelson down to berthing. Deputy Dog was standing by the quarterdeck and as we passed he said, "You better keep him quite or I put him on report." Nelson jumped out of our grasp and maniacally screamed, "YAAAA" in Deputy Dog's face, scaring the hell out of him. All Deputy Dog could say was "God Dom it you fucking ass hoes," and walked away as we laughed at him.

We went down to the berthing area and tried to get Sea Hunt to calm down to hit the rack. No way. The coffee had struck and Sea Hunt was hyper-drunk. Everyone who had been awakened with our noisy entrance, started hollering at us to shut him up. Sea Hunt went nuts and started running up to anyone who was complaining and screamed, "YOU WANT ME TO SHUT THE FUCK UP? YOU SHUT THE FUCK UP!" He got right in their faces until we pulled him off.

We decided that it was off to the dive locker for Sea Hunt. It was now almost 3 a.m. and we dragged Sea Hunt there. He was really freaking out now and talking all kinds off weird stuff.

"Dogs can fuck all night."

"Did you know that pigs have curly penises?

"Whipped cream tastes really good when you lick it off someone's ass."

"There's nothing wrong with me I mean it, I really do mean it."

He kept going on and on. We made the decision without even having to say it. Lock Down for Sea Hunt. We made sure the back door had a key lock on it and the front door locked from the outside. Sea Hunt figured out what we were going to do and made a run for the front door, but he didn't get far. We dragged him back in. He went wild like an animal about to be caged. Because we couldn't shut the door while he was trying to get out, we decided on another alternative. Duct tape was brought out, and with three of us holding him down, West taped his feet together. He was fighting like a mad man and was very hard to hold. We dragged him into the back room and we all ran for the front door. The last thing we heard before slamming the door shut was Sea Hunt's pitiful scream, "NOOOO." He sounded like someone that was being sealed up in his own coffin. We all hit the rack and slept well.

The next morning we went down to see if Sea Hunt was all right. As we opened the door, and there he was, dressed in his greens, with coffee made and reading a magazine at the table. We figured he'd either still be passed out or really pissed off at us. To our shock, he acted like nothing happened at all. We brought up some of the fun events that had happened the night before, excluding all the bullshit that happened on board and he laughed with us, but we could tell that he just didn't remember any of it. Sea Hunt was just a space cadet, that's all there was to it. Senior Chief would come up to us and ask, "Is he on dope?" We'd just shrug our shoulders and say, "We'd like to tell you that he is, but unfortunately he's just that way naturally."

From all the weird stories he heard from the quarterdeck Chief and others, Senior Chief worried about Sea Hunt. He would always give him a good once over when he returned to the boat, and would never let him dive alone.

Chapter 11

Chip Chance-The Evil Richie Cunningham

Chip Chance loved being a diver, but he didn't look like a typical diver...muscular, buff, and spectacular! At about 6'1", skinny as a rail with strawberry-colored hair and freckles, Chip Chance looked like the mischievous Richie Cunningham from TV's Happy Days.

Chip was an army brat. His dad was a highly decorated army officer and was stationed for his last six years in the service, at the Pentagon in Washington, D.C. Chip spent most of his upper school years growing up in Alexandria, Virginia. He was the nightmare of his very disciplined, rigid, career, officer father. Chip had genius-level intelligence, but he seemed to only to use it in ways that would cause vandalism or dirty tricks. He rarely gave any effort in school, but he still received excellent grades. In an attempt to straighten out his son, his father sent him to the Virginia Military Institute for his freshman year of high school. Chip didn't last six months.

This was a letter from the Commandant of the school to Chip's father:

We regret to inform you of the expulsion of your son Chip from the Virginia Military Institute. Your son has been unable to conform to the rigid discipline and academic requirements of our fine institution.

Sincerely,
Commandant Jonathan P. Wilkerson, III

What the Commandant really meant was they couldn't control Chip, and he scared the hell out of them. As was the case for all freshmen, the upperclass men terrorized Chip, but only for a while. Then strange things started happening. Anyone who gave scrubworm Chance a hard time had something bad happen to them.

It was a tradition that upperclassmen had their shoes shined by the worm freshmen. Then, all of the upperclassmen got a mysterious and painful rash on their feet and were barely able to walk, their skin literally peeling off. The connection to Chip was loosely made.

A while later, on the coldest day of winter, a sulfur stink bomb was set off by the main air intake for the heating system of the seniors' dormitory. Rumors had it that Chip was responsible. No proof though.

One night Chip entered the senior dormitory, which was against the rules. However, for Chip, rules were something to ignore if they got in the way of his fun. Chip had stolen a caulking gun from the maintenance shop and proceeded to glue all the doors shut with liquid-nail Super Glue. No one saw him go in or out of the dormitory, but everyone knew who did it. The doors had to be chiseled open and this caused quite a bit of chaos at the Virginia Military Institute.

Chip's tricks weren't always funny. He had an evil side to him too, and anyone who threatened him had this side unleashed on them. All the members of the senior class avoided him like the plague. They were actually afraid of Chip; it was like living with a psycho, the way they talked about him. The final straw for Chip was when he put black gunpowder in the air filter of the Commandant's car and blew the carburetor and hood off his Cadillac Seville. He never got caught, but everyone knew who did it.

After his expulsion from the prestigious military academy, Chip graduated a semester early from a public high school in Alexandria and enlisted in the Navy. This step caused his West Point-graduated father a great deal of stress.

Chip had no problem passing dive school and was assigned to our ship. He'd been a successful diver here for almost three years, by the time I came aboard and joined the diving crew. He'd finally found a place to call home and he seemed to like the Navy and his job.

When we were in Rota, Spain, working on the USS Barney, I had the job of shutting the ship down so we could dive on it for maintenance. To shut a ship down, I had to go to the engineering department to secure (or stop) all the equipment that was near the location where we would be diving. The water was really dirty with almost zero visibility and I had to make sure all the suctions in the area of our work were secured, and the valve handles and on/off switches were chained or wired shut. This was a matter of life or death for us divers. One time we didn't chain the valves and a fire pump on one of the ships was turned on, despite the red danger tags all over the valve. Luckily, we felt the water start moving and got away quickly because with suction at about 1000 gallons per minute the water could have sucked the air right out of our lungs if we had got caught in it.

I walked into the engineering office to have the department head assign me a sailor. Who do I meet? The newly transferred engineering department head, Lt. Hemorrhoid Bunzy.

"Well, look who's here," I said.

"What do you want?" he said, looking at me with disgust.

"I need an engineer to walk me through the shut-down sheet."

"I don't have anybody available right now. Come back in about a half an hour," he said with a smug, "I've-got-the-power" look on his face.

"Fine," I said with a smile on my face, and walked out the door.

I remembered what the Senior Chief told me about getting the job done. If some snively-nosed Junior officer gives you a hard time, go directly to the XO, pass go, and collect $200. So, I knocked on the XO's door and informed him that we wouldn't be working on his ship today, and to reschedule because we weren't getting any cooperation from the engineering officer.

"WHAT? Follow me, Petty Officer Fredrickson," he said after looking at my name tag.

Down to the engineering office we marched. I stood and watched as Hemorrhoid got his ass chewed by the XO.

"Do you know how long it took to get these divers over here to do this work, Lt. Bunzy? Are you going to march into the CO and explain to him, –Sir, we can't get underway because I was much too busy being an asshole to let the divers do the work we requested them to do?' Lt. Bunzy, you will accompany this diver around the ship and personally make sure he has everything he needs to complete his task. IS THAT UNDERSTOOD?"

"Yes, sir."

It couldn't be any sweeter. Bunzy was like my lap dog after that.

While I was getting the shut down complete, Chip was getting the rest of us some lunch from the galley. He went in and talked to the chief Filipino cook and told, not asked, him to make eight box lunches for the dive boat crew. While he was waiting for the lunches, Chip starting snooping around. He went into the bake room and lo and behold, there was a gold-mine. Twenty-five freshly baked apple pies all lined up on the counter, cooling.

Chip started putting the pies in a big box he'd found. He didn't take one or two pies, but grabbed 10. He quickly darted back to the fantail where the dive boat was parked.

"Hey, throw me a line," he yelled down to the boat. West coiled a line up and did his best Cowboy Bob routine and flung the line up to Chip, who quickly tied the box and lowered it down to the dive boat. As soon as the pies were taken out, he pulled the empty box back up and ran back to the galley again. Looking around slyly, he sneaked back into the bake shop and packed up the rest of the pies and again ran back to the dive boat to deposit his booty.

Then, walking slowly back to the galley as if he didn't have a care in the world, Chip entered through a different entrance than the one by the bake shop. The Chief was just starting to look around for him when he walked in.

"Chief, are those lunches ready yet?"

The chief waved him over and pointed to a box with the lunches. Chip did one of his watch-the-left-hand-while-the-right-hand-is-stealing-your-wallet-acts; he said to the chief while pulling out his pocket note book and pen, "How do you spell your name again? A-B-R-I-G-O? Thanks a lot. We'll include your name in our report to the XO about the great cooperation we received from your people."

You could tell by the look on his face that having his name mentioned in the XO's report made the Chief's day. He walked away probably thinking those divers aren't so bad after all.

Chance knew all the buttons to push. He could be your best friend or your worst enemy. Lucky for me, most of the time we got along very well. Now, with Bunzy being my errand boy, I went back to the boat to eat lunch. But instead of eating, Senior Chief decided that we would finish the work on the Barney before we ate lunch. I told Senior Chief about the little run-in with Bunzy and he thought it was real funny. We nicknamed Bunzy, Barney Fife, after the deputy in the old TV program, the Andy Griffith Show.

We were doing our best Barney Fife whiny imitations, "Now Andy, I had those divers just by the short and curlies, and I'd have had 'em hopping like they had fire ants in their pants, if you hadn't stopped me." Before every sentence we said, we would whine, "Now Andy."

Even talking over the comm system, which was now the Mayberry party line, we would use country twang. Everyone took a show name. Senior Chief played the role of Sheriff Andy Taylor. Carter immediately suggested that I would be the faggot, Gomer Pyle. I returned that Carter would be my good butt buddy brother, Goober. Chance was unanimously voted the role of Opie since he looked just like him. Jerry West was Floyd the Barber, Workman was Mr. Drucker the store owner, and Nelson was Otis, the town drunk.

Right when we were going through one of our routines, who should stick his head over the fantail? "Hey, how's it going?" Bunzy called down to Senior Chief. With a look of apprehension on his face. He was really sweating it because of his earlier indiscretion with me and the XO.

"It's going fine. We've just finished up, Lt. Fife," Senior Chief piped back. We all started laughing at his mockery of Lt. Bunzy.

Bunzy didn't get the joke and replied, "That's Lt. Bunzy, Senior Chief. Well, good. Let me know if I can get anything for you."

"Lt. Fife, could you get us some of that pie from the galley," replied Chip. "It looked real good."

Not listening to what Chip had said to him, "I'll see what I can do," Bunzy replied, turning away.

All of us knew he wasn't going to do a damn thing about getting us any pie. What could he do anyway? We all laughed again at Chip's audacity. We all wanted to get out of there quickly before anyone noticed all the pies missing. We moved the boat a pier down to the USS Cunningham for another hull inspection.

The dives on the Cunningham were uneventful and done very quickly. We then drove back to the Puget Sound to clean up our equipment and to finish all the paper work. On the way back, Chance kept flicking pieces of apple pie at Nelson and me.
He was standing by the Senior Chief, who was driving the boat, so there was no way we could retaliate. We still had about 20 pies in the box down in the forward cabin.

After we moored the boat , Senior Chief gave everyone instructions and left for the Goat Locker, which is what we called the Chief's Mess.

Nelson had gone down to the cabin to get another pie and brought the whole box of them up instead. He set them all down by me. As Nelson bent over to get a pie, Chip flicked a big piece of apple and hit Nelson right in the ear. That started it. Sea Hunt went ballistic and grabbed a handful of pie and flung it at Chip. He used the shot gun technique and it accidentally wiped out West and Carter as well.

The pie melee began. Pie flew everywhere and Chip hit me hard in the face with a whole pie, which really hurt. I thought I'd broken my nose because I tasted blood in my mouth. I grabbed a pie tin and cracked him on the side of his head. We were about to go to blows when the voice of God boomed down on us. We all stopped and looked up. Senior Chief had forgotten to tell us something and came out on deck and witnessed the little war.

"You assholes thought you were getting off early today, huh? I want every crumb of that shit cleaned up and you assholes in the dive locker in 30 minutes. Understood?"

After we cleaned up the dive boat, we mustered in the dive locker. It was the general consensus that Chip was responsible for the whole thing and that he should be man enough to admit it to Senior Chief, take the punishment, and let us off the hook.

Senior Chief came in to the dive locker and made us all stand at attention in two rows. We knew he was really pissed when he made us do that. Normally he was pretty kicked back about Navy protocol. Chip did his manly duty and admitted that he was the one who started it.

"Senior Chief, I'm the..." Senior Chief cut him off.

"I know that. Any time stupid shit like that happens, I look to you first. I thought you were all grown men, but I guess I've got a bunch of 12 year olds. I'd just come from the XO's office bragging about you guys and I come out and what do I see? A bunch of adolescent BOYS, reliving their mud pie fight days," and he went on and on. After about five minutes, he lost steam and proceeded to tell us our punishment. After dinner, we were to proceed to the dive boat and scrub the boat bottom and clean the bilge. We were then to report to Senior Chief in our dress blue uniforms at the dive boat for inspection.

The bilges were oily and smelled like diesel fuel. This job sucked. But the worst was cleaning the bottom of the boat where there were a million critters hanging on it. When you scrubbed them off, they always got in your hair, ears, and swim suit. God, it was creepy having little shrimp, sea worms, and mini-crabs crawling around your nuts and butt hole. It always gave me visions that they would borough up one of your holes and lay eggs or something. Of course every new diver heard the story about an eight-foot-long carnivorous leach worm that was pulled out of a diver's crank, while he screamed his lungs out.

Chip kept going up to Nelson and saying, "Man, I feel something's in my crank. Would you look to see if you see something?"

Sea Hunt didn't know how to take this request. The thought of something crawling up his crank really freaked him out, and he was vocal about his concerns. Now that we saw how freaky he was about this, we constantly brought up the subject, again and again. Chip tried that request on me a few months earlier, and I said sure. When I went down to look at it, I whacked the head of his dick as quickly as possible knowing he was going to pee on me, the minute I was in range. Typical diver trick, pee on everything. He howled like I just ripped his wiener off or something. I went around the rest of the day asking him if he needed me to check his crank again.

"I was just killing the worm. You should thank me," I'd say to him.

But Chip kept bugging Sea Hunt about this all the time.

"Goddamn it, Fucking check it yourself," Sea Hunt yelled back on the edge of hysteria, not really knowing how to handle Chip's constant harassment. Chip kept pulling his cock out and wiggling it at Sea Hunt, pretending like something was really inside it.

When Sea Hunt wasn't looking, Workman handed Chip a three to four inch worm he pulled off one of the pilings on the pier. Chip started a painful, spastic dance, moaning real loud. He had his cock in his hand and started screaming, "There's something in it, there's something in it. OH GO-O-O-D!"

Chip yelled in agony and dropped to his knees, making it look like he was pulling the worm out of the head of his penis. Collapsing on the boat deck, Chip rocked back in forth in waves of pain that racked his body. His charade slowly subsided.

We knelt down by Chip to inspect the worm and to comfort him. I said to Sea Hunt Nelson in a very serious voice, "If you had just checked him, this wouldn't have happened. Dear God, he probably won't be able to father any children any more."

All of us stared with a hard look at Sea Hunt, and he looked so pitiful and guilty. He had an anguished look on his face like a kid whose puppy just got killed and it was his fault. Chip was still quietly whimpering in seemingly horrible pain, but we couldn't keep it up. Finally Chip got up and broke the moment, "Fuck Nelson, you are one stupid, gullible mother fucker aren't you. I thought you were going to cry there for a minute."

We all started laughing and Sea Hunt was embarrassed, yet relieved. He was not the quickest human being on earth, and was still trying to figure out the meaning of all the events that had just taken place. He still had a bewildered look on his face.

Now it was time to go back to work. We knew the jobs, with all of us working together, would only take about an hour to do. We also knew that Senior Chief wanted to see a show in a nightclub in Rota, Spain, with this really hot Senorita singer in it. Senior Chief never screwed off on his wife, but he liked to look, think and talk about it a lot. So, if we delayed, and made him late for his 20:00 show, we didn't want to think about the consequences of that.

We made Chip clean the worst part of the bilges and finish cleaning the keel of the boat. We reported for inspection in our dress blues. Senior Chief checked us out and the boat in his civilian clothes, and dismissed us.

After Senior Chief left, we were all standing around the deck of the diving boat when unbeknownst to Chip, Sea Hunt Nelson had hidden a pie down in the front storage space. We were still pissed at Chip for his part in starting the pie fight. Sea Hunt got the last pie out of its hiding place. Just as Chip was getting ready to leave the boat, Carter grabbed him and held him in a bear hug. We then stripped him down to his underwear and tee shirt and Sea Hunt pulled open the top of his shorts and dumped the entire pie down the front of his skivvies. We then tossed him down the forward hold and closed the door and held it shut until everyone was off the boat. We took his uniform with us and told him we would lower it down from the ship after we all got on board.

Sea Hunt had the power of the uniform and called down to Chip as he lowered his uniform to him. The rest of us stood next to him on the fantail of the ship.

"Hey Chip, need a little ice cream with your hair pie?" Sea Hunt Nelson blasted out a hysterically insane laugh like some mad scientist. He kept it up as he was lowering Chip's uniform to him. As the uniform was nearly in his reach, Sea Hunt faked like he slipped and dropped his uniform nearly in the water. Chip screamed out as his dress uniform was nearly dunked in the nasty bay water, and Sea Hunt caught it just in time.

"I-----I gotcha!"

Mike "Sea Hunt" Nelson was the happiest man alive, because he finally had the last laugh on Chip Chance.

Chapter 12

Garbage From Heaven

Our ship had been idly sitting off the coast of Lebanon for 38 days. Everyone was getting edgy and irritable about it too. We were here to support any land operations that might need our help. Nothing much was happening until one day the order to evacuate all civilian personnel from the Beruit Embassy came through and we were to be involved. Politically, things were beginning to heat up in Beruit. Boredom to combat in less than 12 hours.

The evacuation helicopters were deployed from the nearby helo-carrier ship and a pilot rescue swimmer was needed to accompany them. Because I was the only diver who had taken the pilot survival course, I was to ride along in one of the choppers as they flew in and out of the bombed and smoking city of Beruit. This was an actual combat mission and I was really nervous. This was even more clear to me when our chopper's pilot explained the safety procedures in case we crashed.

"All right everyone, if we go down in the water, it's every man for himself. The chopper sinks in less than 30 seconds, so get out fast, and then try to help other people. Any questions? Okay, let's go."

Looking out the window on the city below, the sounds of mortars and rocket explosions made my heart pound. The smoke billowed up from many sections of the city that were on fire. We flew in low, quickly landed, took on embassy personnel, and got the hell out of there – fast! Luckily, each chopper was only in the hot zone for about 15 minutes on each evacuation run. I was afraid that some radical Arab with a shoulder missile launcher would hear Allah's command to purify the skies of infidels, and blow us up. Allah must have been sleeping that day because all choppers got in and out safely. By the end of the day, we had made 12 runs, and all the civilian personnel had been removed from the Beirut Embassy.

I was so glad to rejoin my diving team and get back to the safety of working among the propellers and other moving parts on the ship's hull at a 30-foot depth. With combat experience behind me, I reaffirmed that I had chosen the right path in the Navy. Below the water was better than above.

Our ship was only one among the mighty U.S. fleet. Our awesome presence offshore was enough to probably restrain much of what the Arabs might have done. Force is a deterrent, and our visibility was a definite show of US strength. Some of the ships had been stationed off the Lebanese coast now for more than 90 days, and many of them needed major repairs. As fleet tenders, we started working open ocean on them. These orders came 12 hours after I had stepped out of the evacuation chopper.

Working open ocean had only one big problem. All the ships dumped their garbage over the side which attracted all kinds of scavenger fish, including some very big sharks. At first it wasn't too bad having to work among all this sea life. But on one fateful day, this changed.

Workman and I were down working on one of the amphibious helicopter carriers. These ships are mini aircraft carriers and very tall; 60 feet from deck to water's surface. Their height often deterred a clear view of what was happening directly below in the water, unless you leaned way over the railing. On this memorable day, trash call was announced, and garbage from the last meal is thrown over the side.

During the changing of the watch, the officer of the quarterdeck had forgotten to remind the relief officer that divers would be working over the side. When divers are working, nothing is to be thrown over the side of the ship. Our dive boat was parked at the stern of the carrier and Workman and I were working on one of the screws, deep below the surface. We were blissfully involved in our duties and unaware of anything topside.

Whoosh! Splat! Whoosh! Splat!

Bags of garbage started flying off the end of the ship. It was the mess cooks' job to throw the trash over the side, and they were trying to get it done as fast as possible. Four mess cooks were in a line throwing large garbage bags over the side into the water 60 feet below one after another.

Whoosh! Splat! Whoosh! Splat!

When the flying trash began, the mess cooks couldn't hear the divers on the dive boat below yelling at them, because they had a boom box on deck and were blasting Steve Miller's song, "Fly Like An Eagle." Every time a bag went over the side they'd yell, "Fly like an eagle."

Down below on the dive boat, all hell broke loose. Garbage bags were hitting the dive boat with explosive force, splitting open and sliming the deck and anything and everybody they hit. All the guys ran down below deck dodging the scum shrapnel. A bag hit the communications box, knocking it off the top of our dive boat, breaking off both communication connectors from our hoses.

Underwater, Workman and I continued our work, completely unaware of what was happening topside. We were cutting and unwrapping miles of 1/4" line from the shaft and propeller of the carrier. Loud impact noises started echoing through the water down to us. It sounded like someone doing cannonballs in a swimming pool.

"Hey what's happening up there?" Workman asked me.

When I didn't respond to him, he signaled that the communication system wasn't working, because neither of us could hear each other talk anymore. In a way, that was pretty good because Workman liked to sing while he was working, and that was about annoying as it can get, especially because the only songs he knew were from Abba and Bread, two pansy-ass musical groups that were hated by all the of the hard-core, rock-and-roll-loving divers. Here was a huge, massively strong, fearless guy with a reputation for severely kicking butt, preferring to listen to girlie music – and singing it too. It didn't fit, but no one pressed the issue too far with him.

We had enough experience diving together to have developed a sign language system that was almost as good as talking. I signed, "Give them line pull signals." Workman proceeded to initiate the diver's secondary communication system. Divers have been trained to send short to-the-point signals by pulling on their diving hose. Every signal must be returned by the tender on topside, so the diver knows that the tender received the correct signal.

First, Workman sent "answer the phone." When nothing happened, he sent the "okay" signal. No response. The cannonball sounds from above continued at a steady pace. He then gave the signal that we were "coming up." Still no response. This was very unusual. No communication at all with us. As we started to put away our tools, we noticed chunks of garbage starting to float all around us. Both of us looked at each other and knew instantly what was going on. An aerial attack from the friendlies. We signaled each other that we should wait safely underwater until it was over.

After about a minute, we noticed that small fish were starting to swarm all around the bits of food that filled the water. The fish swarms grew bigger and bigger in size and quantity. Then, a huge school of mullet, about 12 to 18 inches long, came flying in, scattering the small fish. The mild feeding frenzy started. Workman and I entertained ourselves by watching this spectacle. There were thousands of fish, and not one of them ran into us. Their ability to maneuver was amazing. They always managed to turn at the last second and dart away.

Moments later, we started noticing a much bigger shadow: three-to-four-foot-long white tip sharks charging through the masses of fish. At first we saw just a few. Then, there was a school of more than 100 sharks coming closer and closer. It got worse when the real big "daddies" started rolling in. Several 10 foot tiger sharks started lunging and biting anything they could get their teeth on. The blood, fish parts, and confusion swirled and churned and we were in the middle, helpless.

Workman and I didn't have to think twice about our odds of survival here. We had a choice between being eaten by a pack of frenzied sharks, or getting hit by a bag of vicious garbage. Decision made, up we went, as quickly and controlled as possible. The garbage bags luckily had stopped coming. We found out later that this was due to Senior Chief Ludwig, who had crawled out from below deck and found the flare gun, shooting an emergency smoke signal 60 feet above, staring at the garbage-covered dive boat and shark feeding frenzy below.

All the crew on the diving boat quickly came topside, shocked at the mess and at the chaos in the water. West immediately checked the communication box and saw the broken connections. He and Carter grabbed the diving hose and frantically tried to get a strain on the line so they could give line pull signals. The water was very clear and all they could see was a churning mass of sea life in this bubbling, bloody riot. In panic, they kept pulling in the line as quickly as possible when our fists popped to the surface, followed by our heads. We were about 15 feet from the dive boat. West and Carter reeled us in like large fish on lines. Our dive team shouted encouragement, but there was sheer panic in their voices. Workman and I barely touched the water and seemed to fly as we were pulled up so hard and fast. Senior Chief Ludwig was expecting two dead or very injured men as we flopped onto the deck. Our dive hats were taken off and Workman and I gave the standard "Divers on deck, divers okay" signal loud and clear. Relief was expressed all around.

We slipped off our fins and unhooked our safety belts and jumped up, whooping and howling like we'd just won the world's shark fighting championship. The blood-brown water around the dive boat still churned with garbage, voracious sharks, and fish bodies.

"It's a world's championship," we yelled and jumped like madmen. We just swam through the most heart-thumping experience of our lives, with our balls still hanging where they should be. After the commotion died down a bit, the next matter to deal with was the trash issue. We had never seen Senior Chief Ludwig so worked up. He said that he had visions of pulling up the diving hoses with nothing but empty safety belts attached. His guts were churning as he waited to see if Workman and I hit the surface. When everything was secure on deck he said in a steady voice, "Take me to the boat landing and wait off for me."

Senior Chief was normally a pretty kicked-back kind of guy. After two tours in Vietnam, nothing seemed to phase him, but now his jaw was set and his eyes were beady and focused. Usually he'd be driving the boat, but now his only thoughts were getting his hands on the idiot who gave the near-fatal order to dispose of the garbage.

Carter smoothly pulled the dive boat up to the ramp stairs that led up to the quarterdeck. Senior Chief was up the steps in seconds. The boat pulled off as the Senior Chief had ordered. This also gave us all a better vantage point to view what would be going on. West picked up the Senior Chief in the binoculars and gave the blow-by-blow account like a sports announcer.

"Ludwig's wagging his finger at what looks like a little ensign. He's poking him in the chest and the wimp is backing up. Now he's got him by the arm and dragging him aft. Quick, pull the boat aft."

About one minute later on the fantail, the Senior Chief Ludwig and the hapless ensign showed up again. The feeding frenzy in the water around us had slowed a little, but there was still plenty of garbage and large sea life. The word had spread quickly on the carrier about the sharks and the fantail was packed with gawking sailors. Carter pulled the boat close to the fantail and Ludwig was picked up again in the binoculars, with West continuing his report.

"Ludwig's still hollering at him. This one's easy, I can read his lips: How'd you like to go swimming with the sharks like my guys, you fucking asshole."

The ensign was scared white because he might have just ruined his naval career. Ludwig started to loudly count the errors that had been committed:

1) Not checking the back log in the watch book and trusting the off-going watch to provide all the information;
2) Not announcing "divers working over the side," which related to error number one;
3) Ordering the trash call early without permission.

The third error related to error number one, because the ensign wouldn't have done it if he'd read the log and knew that divers were working below. One error led to the next. This ensign was screwed.

There were more than 100 sailors watching Ludwig ream the ensign, and some were openly laughing. Maybe going for a swim among the sharks wouldn't be half as bad when compared to what the carrier's Captain would do to this ensign later.

Our boat was waiting for Ludwig when he arrived at the bottom of the ramp. We picked him up and returned to the Puget Sound.

"Boy, I wish we had the UDATS video camera going. That would have been an awesome video," Workman declared. "Can you imagine all those fish and those big daddies rolling in there, right around my shoulders. I'd send it home to my mom. Yo, mom, just another working dive. She'd shit."

When we returned to our ship, we tied up to our mooring and stowed all the boat gear. A hose was sent down with scrub brushes to clean off the slimy mess splattered all over. "Wow, this stuff stinks," Nelson complained, as he and Workman, the two lowest-ranking guys, scrubbed away the slimy mess. West, Carter, and I maintenanced the diving helmets and repaired the communication connections. We all had worked up a powerful appetite from the day's happenings. It was chow time.

Chapter 13

Does Your Food Smell?

The food on the USS Puget Sound was a daily adventure, depending on who the head cook was. Most of the cooks were Filipino and learned to cook from English recipe cards. They had no idea what real Italian, Southern, Mexican, or American cooking tasted like, only what the card told them to do. Filipino foods such as adobo, lumpia, or fried rice, were excellent. If it wasn't Filipino food, it was known as "Filipino surprise" because what it said on the menu wasn't at all what we were served.

One of the rules of the mess deck was to guard your tray or have a trusted ally watch it for you at all times if you had to get up for something in the middle of your meal. The reason for this buddy system was that sailors loved to mess with each other's food. Hence, a mess deck.

We had just finished cleaning up the garbage slime from our dive boat and went as a group to get supper before it was too late. We were famished, exhausted from dodging flying garbage and surviving shark attacks, and a good hot meal seemed just the thing to calm us down. It was towards the end of chow when we actually got our meal, and finding enough vacant seats was tough. Our regular seats were taken, and the only table with enough places was the R-5 Electronic Technician's table. We all sat there – even though it was foreign territory.

Workman sat down next to ET2 Parks, who looked over at Workman and gave him a vicious look. "This isn't your table. Go find some place else to sit." Parks was about 6' 5", 250 lbs. and intimidated most of the other sailors on the ship. He earned a reputation as a real shit kicker after a few beers.

Workman looked over at Parks, eye to eye, and said, "That's nice," and went back to eating his dinner. Through the whole meal we ignored Parks, who kept up a loud monologue about his distaste for divers and his "no fear" attitude toward them. "Fucking divers think they're hot shit. But all they really are is shit," and variations on that theme.

We acted like he wasn't even there. This infuriated Parks even more. After about 15 minutes, Workman and I got up and went to the dessert area and picked up six pieces of cake. One for each diver, and Workman gave a piece of cake to Parks who begrudgingly said, "Thanks."

All the divers waited and Workman cut into his cake, which looked pretty tasty. It was a three-inch-tall white cake with thick white frosting. He took a big bite and after chewing it for a while, made a face as if he'd eaten something that tasted foul.

"Wow, that's terrible," he said and bent over and sniffed the cake closely, making a face again. All of us bent over and sniffed our cake too, making faces of disgust. Workman turned to Parks and asked, "Does yours smell funny too?"

Everyone else had bent over and sniffed, which was the standard trick to help lure victims to get their faces closer to their food. Then as they bent down to smell it, someone would push their face into the food. It was funny as hell.

Workman turned to get into position to help Parks get a good sniff, but Parks didn't bend down to smell his cake. Parks instead, picked up his plate and brought it up to his face to get an even better sniff. This was a dream come true. As Parks sniffed his cake, Workman smashed the plate and Parks face together in a quick clapping motion, one hand under the plate and the other on the back of Park's head.

The cake was mashed over Park's wide face. The plate dropped away but the cake and frosting stuck to his face. Workman was looking at him with a straight face. Parks reached up and slowly wiped the cake from his eyes. Workman asked in an innocent voice, "Well, does your cake stink too?"

The mess decks roared with the laughter of more than 500 sailors. Parks exploded, jumped up from his chair, and yelled, "I'm gonna kick your ass!"

Workman stood up calmly and faced Parks, who continued yelling threats at him. Workman just stared at him for a few seconds. Then in a loud and deadly sounding voice, "Either do something or shut up and sit down."

Looking around the mess deck, Parks saw that everyone was eager for some action and waiting for his next move. Normally when he threatened someone, they would act scared. What he saw in Workman appeared to unnerved him. Cold; blue deadly eyes, with not an ounce of fear.

It was obvious that Parks was becoming embarrassed, and scared himself. Parks screamed out, "You're on report," and ran up the ladder behind him to find security at the Master-at-Arms office. Unfortunately for Parks, when he arrived at the MAA's office he was met by the smiling face of BM 1 Benunni.

Parks filled out his report detailing all the disrespect and assault charges he could think to bring against Workman. As Parks was writing out his report chit, Benunni received a phone call from me, detailing all the other things that happened that Parks had failed to reveal in his version. When Parks was done writing his report, he handed it to Benunni and started to leave.

"Wait a minute Parks. I need to go over the details of the report so I understand exactly what happened. Now, under the assault charge, did he hit you with his hands?

"Well, no."

"A weapon then?"

"Ah, he hit me with a piece of cake."

"So, let's put under action, 'Victim assaulted with piece of vanilla cake'."

Benunni was trying very hard to keep a straight face while visualizing Workman doing the stinking food trick on this big idiot. He also thought it was a waste of a perfectly good piece of cake and was starting to get kind of hungry thinking about it. He made a mental note to go down after this and check out the assault weapon.

"Is that right?" Benunni questioned.

Becoming embarrassed at the direction this was going, Parks' anger was quickly fading.

"Okay, let's put this all together the way the Captain would look at it and, most of all, the way the other witnesses would see it. 'HT-3 Workman, reacting to repeated taunting and verbal threats unprovoked by him, retaliated by assaulting ET 2 Parks with a tasty piece of vanilla cake.'"

Benunni waited a few seconds to let it sink in and with a smirk on his face added, "Son, are you sure you really want to file this report and embarrass yourself more?"

After a few more seconds and no answer from Parks, Benunni continued, "Tell you what, why don't you go get cleaned up and think about it for awhile and if you decide to continue with this, it will be right here waiting for you." Parks turned and walked away without answering. Benunni knew he wasn't going to come back and threw the report in the trash can, chuckling to himself.

Parks had now acquired the new nickname "Sniffer," the only man alive capable of eating cake through his nose and able to sniff out foul odors from miles away.

Sailors would go up to the door of Parks' repair shop and ask, "Hey, what's for lunch?"

"How the fuck am I suppose to know?" Parks would answer.

"Gee, I figured you could smell it from here," and the sailor would quickly leave, before Parks could tear after him.

Chapter 14

Green Meat

The food got progressively worse as the ship waited off the coast of Lebanon. It finally came to a head one evening at dinner. There was only one choice for the entree that night – beef stew. As we waited in line, something just didn't smell right.

The mess deck was full of hundreds of sailors and the grumbling started. It was like a wave that built slowly and intensely until it crashed on shore. Scores of sailors started to bring back the stew because it smelled so foul. After witnessing the Parks incident and the cake sniffing, no crew member was caught too long sniffing their putrid entree. Pulling the stinking food trick again would have to wait until a few more new guys checked on board. Line after line of guys, trays in hand, filed past the mess tables, fiercely depositing their trays.

The Filipino cooks claimed innocence saying that they were ordered to use the stew meat by their department head. This didn't satisfy anyone. Now trays were being thrown back into the kitchen through the chow line window. The cooks could feel the hostility increasing and called the MAA's office. No one answered their 911 call and, in a panic, they called their department head.

The mess decks were getting ugly. There is one rule about managing 1,600 sailors on board a large ship: keep them well fed with good food! Hungry sailors are trouble waiting to happen. We were having a lot of fun with this, though. We would start chants which would be picked up by each section of tables, passing it around until the entire crew was booming in unison. It sounded pretty dangerous!

"The food sucks! The food sucks" over and over again.

"Green meat! Green meat!"

"Throw it back! Throw it back!"

The chanting got so enthusiastic that it sounded like a high school pep rally at a football game. Every once in awhile, meat would fly across the mess decks. When the din was at its peak, Supply Department Head Commander Worthington came down the ladder from officer's country onto the mess deck.

Worthington was 6' 5" tall and had an arrogant and condescending attitude towards enlisted personnel. In a loud and commanding voice he bellowed, "What is the meaning of this disturbance?" He looked around, angry that anyone would question his decision to serve any of his food. He acted like anything that was brought on board the ship through his supply department was his personal property. Worthington took this revolt personally.

Electricians Mate Fireman Dorner stood up bravely and said, "This stew sucks. Sir."

Everyone yelled and cheered, "Ya-a-a-a-a."

"There's nothing wrong with this stew," he declared.

"Are you crazy? It stinks. And look, the meat's green."

"I'm telling you, there's nothing wrong with it!" he said with even more force, glaring at the small insignificant seaman complaining before him.

"If it's so good, then you eat it. Sir."

The loudness of the cheering and the anger set Commander Worthington back.

The chant, "Eat it! Eat it!" was started by the divers.

Worthington finally gathered himself together and yelled, "All right! Give me that tray." Looking at everyone staring at him in wild anticipation, he took a large bite of beef stew.

"More! More!" started the chant.

He took one more large bite, swallowed, and angrily declared, "There's nothing wrong with this stew!" He then looked at Dorner and said, "You're on report for disrespect, sailor. Be at my office at 1900 hours to sign your report chit."

He turned and went up the ladder, back to officer's country.

Within seconds after he left, someone yelled, "Fuck him," and the food started flying. The duty MAA came on the mess decks to restore order. Unfortunately for him, it was Deputy Dog, who now became the target of everyone's beef stew. One thousand hungry and angry sailors threw their stew at him from utensil slingshots. Deputy Dog looked like a shooting gallery duck. Every time he'd run one way, he'd get ambushed by several splats of stew, and when he ran the other way, he was clobbered even more. He stood in the middle of the mess deck, beaten and cowering. He curled up in a fetal ball on the deck until everyone mercifully ran out of stew. He looked like a slime ball.

Everyone left, hungry and mad, leaving a huge pigsty in their wake. The poor mess cooks waited for everyone to leave and then started the thankless job of cleaning up after the crew's fury.

At 1900 hours, Dorner showed up, as ordered at Commander Worthington's office, ready to take his punishment. At 1930 hours, Dorner got tired of waiting and found some paper and taped a note on the door, saying he had been waiting and he would be in berthing if the Commander wanted him. It was later reported, through the grapevine, that Worthington was inside his stateroom, retching his guts out in front of the porcelain throne. Someone heard him through his door crying, "Oh god, please not again. Please!! URRUPP..... not again. URRUPP...."

As reported later by the duty corpsman in the Medical Department, just as Worthington was about to do his duty as a commissioned officer and put the insubordinate little worm, Dorner, on report, his stomach started to cramp up. Then he began to bloat and barely made it to the toilet in time. By 2000 hours, he was feverish and staggered to the Medical Department, only to be confronted by 21 other sailors who had unfortunately eaten the stew as well. Looking pale and feeling clammy, he moved to the front of the line, using his rank to be the next one seen by the duty corpsman.

HM 2 John W. Tenworth was the cutest and sweetest little corpsman the Navy ever had. He was giving Bi-cillin shots to all the sailors exposed to the rancid, bacteria-infested stew. To him, this situation of having all these helpless men pull down their pants and bend over, at his command, was a dream come true.

Everyone thought Tenworth was gay. He was small, skinny, and had a very delicate manner and his hometown was San Francisco. He was an excellent corpsman and performed very well under stress during medical emergencies. Because of his skill under fire, he had earned the respect of all who worked with him.

Tenworth also had a good sense of humor. One of the jokes Tenworth liked to play was when he'd check someone's throat. He'd always tell a sailor to close his eyes, open wide, and put a tongue depressor in his mouth. Then he'd tell him to swallow. After he was through examining the throat, it never seemed to feel rough or sore anymore – and no tongue depressor was ever seen. Tenworth always seemed to be smiling after these exams. The warning was: Don't close your eyes.

Tenworth had been down on the mess decks and witnessed the arrogant and rude behavior of Commander Worthington. Now was his chance to get even on behalf of the entire crew.

"Sir, could you please take your pants down and bend over? I'll need to take a stool sample to see if the bacteria has transferred to your colon."

The Commander was too sick to protest the illogic of this request, and only wanted to get fixed up as quickly as possible. Tenworth put a cold, stainless steel test tube on his finger, lubricated it and proceeded to vigorously shove it up the Commander's rectum. At the touch of the cold stainless steel tube going up his ass, Worthington jumped, forcing Tenworth to push the tube in even harder. The Commander let out a whimpering yelp as the tube went in another four inches. Tenworth then pulled the tube out and repeated the procedure again. Worthington was in agony.

"Ah-h-h, I got a good sample that second time," Tenworth said. "Now I'm going to give you two shots of antibiotics. One in each cheek of your buttocks. You'll feel a little pinch and then you can be on your way."

Only one shot was actually needed, but two would give the Commander a really painful butt for about two days. The Bi-cillin was a thick serum and always caused a big knot in the muscle. If you received one shot, you could avoid the extremely painful cheek and sit on the other one, but by administering shots in both cheeks, excruciating pain would have to be endured.

The Commander left after his shots and went to his stateroom. Tenworth was the hero of the day throughout the ship when he passed the word around about what he did. Gay or not, he was one of the guys, and his revenge on Worthington elevated him even further in our eyes.

The next morning Worthington was back in medical, not for food poisoning, but for a cut and a large lump on his head. In his fevered delirium the night before, he rolled onto his back and the pain in his butt sent two electric shock waves through his body. He reared up in his bunk and slammed his head against the overhead light, nearly knocking himself out. He landed on his painful butt again, twisting in agony, then fell out of bed ramming his elbow hard on the steel floor.

Thus, Commander Green Meat's legend began. Dorner was never put on report. Worthington still wanted to take it out on the insubordinate worm, Dorner, just to save face, but the XO wisely quieted the incident down. The commander was sick for three days and when he didn't show up for work, the rumor was that he'd died and anyone else who had touched the green meat stew was sure to follow.

Just like the popular TV commercial phrase during that time, "Give it to Mikey; he'll eat anything," whenever a menu item tasted lousy or was even suspected of being lousy, the chow line chant would demand the services of the royal food tester. "Give it to Commander Green Meat; he'll eat anything."

Chapter 15

Stone Head

Casey Carter was from some small hick town in Texas. He checked on board when we arrived in Rota, Spain, after our Atlantic crossing from Norfolk, Virginia.

Casey was 6' 3" and weighed about 240 lbs. He had a large barrel chest and about 20" arms. He was the most typical slow-talking, tobacco-chewing, redneck good ol' boy you'd ever want to meet. He had a head that literally looked like it was carved out of Stone, and gave him that chiseled caveman look. We immediately hated each other from the moment we shook hands and introduced ourselves.

The opening line of greeting started out like this after he was informed that I was from California.

"So, you're from California, right? Are you a faggot?" He slowly drawled, laughing.

"Hold on a minute, Carter. I need to turn my brain to southern half speed, so I can be on your wavelength." Reaching up I turned my ear making a clicking noise. And, speaking very slowly in a mock southern accent, I said, "Now, that's better. By the way, why do you ask? Do you want to suck my dick or something? I might not be as good as a Hefer, but I'll do."

His smile vanished immediately.

That was just the beginning.

Casey was a chewer and left disgusting spit cups all around the dive locker. To have a cup full of tobacco spit spill on you, or have to clean up someone else's spilled chew spit cup pissed all the non-chewers off to no end. I was a non-chewer and was very vocal that the chewers had better stop the irresponsible practice of spit cup abandonment or else revenge would have to be taken.

We were diving on the aircraft carrier U.S.S. America, doing a suction grating cover, so they could work on the pump inside the ship and a hull inspection. Carter and I had been going at it all day with the southern dummy-California faggot smack on each other.

Whenever I talked to Carter, I always did my dumb southerner accent unless Senior Chief hollered at me to stop it.

I was the diver and Carter and West were the tenders hatting and unhatting me on many dive operations. We had to move the boat inbetween dives and Carter kept spitting tobacco spit on my wet suit. Just before I'd enter the water, he'd spit on my face mask. It didn't thrill me to get spit on, but considering I was diving in sewage water outside Naples Harbor, I let it go. As soon as I hit the water it washed off, anyway.

While I was waiting for Carter and West to put my diving hat on, I called out in a southern accent, "Yo bo-o-y, shuffle them feet a little quicker, we're wasting daylight on you trying to figger out which hand to pick up that hose with." Imitating Carter, I pretended to pick up the hose and, stopping halfway and changing hands back and forth, I said "Left, no, right, no, left, no, right." Then I looked up and scratched my head with a bewildered look on my face. The other guys laughed, which pissed Carter off.

"Knock the shit off and get in the water, Fredrickson."

"It's kind of hard to get in Senior Chief without my hat on." I responded, looking at my tenders and shaking my head sadly, with a "they're-so-incompetent" look on my face.

"I'll show you how fucking easy it is to get in the water without your fucking dive hat," said Carter with an evil look on his face.

"I said knock the shit off," Senior Chief yelled in annoyance.

On my last dive for this job, Carter thought he was going to be real funny and spit **in** my mask just before hatting me. He saved up a large mouth full of Redman Chewing tobacco spit and released his load into the hood of the mask. The mask was put on and tobacco spit ran down my face. He then pushed me in the water so I couldn't get the mask off for a while longer.

He howled and drawled through the comm. box "Now, that's the funniest thing I've ever seen. A California faggot covered in redneck spit. It doesn't get any better than this."

I swam back to the dive boat and took off my mask and washed it out with Carter looking over the side pretending to spit more on me.

In the afternoon it was Carter's turn to dive. As he was about to enter the water to do a hull inspection, I called over to him. With diving hat and fins on and tools in hand he turned to watch me pissing in his boots. I then took his uniform pants and put my cock in the back pocket with his wallet in it and finished my release. He screamed and tried to run after me with his fins on across the dive boat.

Casey wasn't the only chewing cup offender. I announced that any chewing cup found unattended would be asking for disposal any means that I saw fit. West stepped into a boot full of spit once. Sea Hunt had a pants pocket full. But my favorite one was Carter. He got in my face and threatened to royally kick my ass if I pulled one of those stunts on him. That was all the motivation I needed. I found Carter's green uniform hat and pulled the paper towel liner he put under the rim to soak up his sweat and poured the spit into it and put it back in the hat rim. We were in a hurry and Carter didn't check his hat. It was a hot day and Carter sweated a lot. As he sweated, brown streaks started to run down his face.

Sea Hunt, who didn't have clue what was going on, looked at Carter and said, "What the hell is all over your face?"

Carter reached up and wiped some of the brown sweat off his forehead and looked bewildered for a second. Then he smelled it. He took his hat off and saw the brown stained towel in the rim of his hat and looked up with a vicious expression on his face.

"Wow, it is true what they say about Rednecks. They do have shit for brains, but it looks like yours are leaking out," I laughed.

He started after me but Senior Chief stopped him.

"I'll get you, you little faggot motherfucker," he screamed.

Wow Deja vu. Where had I heard that one before?

That was the end of the chew wars, because Senior Chief outlawed chewing in the dive locker. Unlucky for West, he knocked a spit cup over and it got on his pants and shoes. West had the privilege to clean the dive boats' oily bilges for his thoughtless mistake. The chew wars might have ended, but that didn't end Carter's and my personal battle.

When our schedule allowed it, we did physical training in the hanger bay. We did everything from weight lifting to wrestling. I was the most experienced, having wrestled from junior high through college along with some international bouts. Everyone would come and watch us go at it in the morning. I was undefeated so far, so I was the one to beat.

Carter was a football lineman and had the mentality of one. He would do the bull run and at 240 lbs. he was amazingly quick. Our first encounter on the mat was a very pleasant one for me.

While in college, one of my wrestling teammates was a judo and Greco-Roman wrestler – a three-time California state champ who ended up at UCLA doing very well in the NCAA tournaments. Wrestling with him for two years taught me a lot about throws and using weight movement against opponents. Carter's only attack method was to charge and grab or tackle. This was real easy to avoid. After he got a little tired, I would come in close and let him grab me. Depending on what he did I either "hip threw" him or "lateral threw" him on the mat. I couldn't hold him down for long because he was just too big and strong.

After he became more weary of charging, I started my next attack method. I tied up with him and every time he would try and grab me, I'd hold the inside of his huge arms and head butt him in the chest. I did this several times and his chest started to hurt, which pissed him off even more. The faggot was hurting him in addition to embarrassing him.

He fell for the setup. As I faked another head butt he flinched back and I ducked under his arm behind him, lifted him up, and slammed him down to the mat. He was stunned at first. I took advantage of this by announcing, "I love it when my girl gets rough, and plays hard to get." I started humping on Carter's ass in mock ecstasy, shouting out, "Oh Baby, oh-h-h, ride em cowboy." He went berserk. After he finally got me off of him – he chased me all around the hanger bay. The whole time he was chasing me, I kept up a constant monologue. "Oh Casey, I know you want more but you have to ask nicely. I'm not that easy. Preparation H will help the itching and swelling and calm down this irritable mood you're in." Again, I was saved by the Senior Chief, who came up to get us all back to work.

Throughout the day, I blew kisses to Casey on the dive boat. Lucky for me, I wasn't the diver that day. I never turned my back on him or let him out of my sight.

Just a few days after this, I found out I had made Second Class Petty Officer (E-5). There was a Navy tradition that when you made a higher rank everyone of equal or higher enlisted rank would come up to you and tack the rank on to your arm. This usually meant a light tap and a handshake. Some of the more sadistic guys would hit pretty hard. Casey was one rank ahead of me and now I was equal in rank to him.

He came up to me and grabbed my arm and lined up to really whack me. A lot of the guys pretended they were going to really nail me but after winding up and swinging hard they would stop just short and tap my arm. Well, Carter swung as hard as he could and hit me in the arm with all his force. The pain shot through me all the way down to my feet. I almost fell just from the shock going through my muscles.

The only thing that saved me was seeing Casey's stupid grinning face. My body went on automatic: "when in pain, attack what's causing the pain". I swung with a hard left hook and two solid straight rights to his smiling face. I didn't get the effect I thought I would, considering that I hit him as hard as I could. He grunted loudly after being knocked back about three or four feet. He then shook his head, cleared it, and came after me. I sprinted out the Diving Locker door and ran down the passageway with Carter chasing after me. He was screaming his standard, "You faggot motherfucker, I'm gonna kil-l-l you."

I lost him very quickly. My arm swelled up almost twice the size of normal and was quickly turning purple-black. I went up to see Butt-licker Brian Horowitz, the Jewish dick-smith corpsman, to have him look at my arm. He freaked out when he saw it. I had an ice bag on it for the next two hours. I could barely move my arm the next day. Casey ended up getting two weeks extra duty from Senior Chief because I couldn't dive during that time.

Our final confrontation came during the ship's full contact karate tournament. The rules were:

1) Three one-minute rounds.
2) Two knock downs end the fight.
3) No kicking in the balls.

We wore head gear, padded boxing jocks, foot kicking pads, and boxing gloves. Casey went through the upper bracket very quickly. Most of the guys he fought were scared shitless of him already and didn't put up much of a fight. Casey had a very good right roundhouse kick, enough to kick every guy he faced down and out in the first round in his first six fights. His only second round came against a boxer named Koontz who kept jabbing and moving for a round and a half, but then he got caught with a big roundhouse kick and it was over.

I ended up going the distance in four of my seven fights but none of them were really very close. Two of the guys were pretty big and, with gloves on, I couldn't get enough power to put them down – no matter how many times I hit them.

The finals – David Against Goliath the Grudge Match – were wild. Anybody who knew us was aware this was going to be a full-on war with no prisoners taken. The crowd couldn't have asked for more.

The crowd was thundering with about 1,500 guys crammed all around the fantail and upper decks of the ship.

As a repair ship, we had the means to manufacture just about anything, so we built an aluminum-plated boxing ring. It was about four feet off the deck and measured 16' square. The ring posts and deck were covered with pads made in the sail shop and the ropes were brand new nylon mooring lines. The ring was beautiful.

We came out to the center of the ring and faced off with the referee. The finals were three, two-minute rounds. Big guys get tired faster.

"I'm gonna put a hurt'en on you, Faggot," said Carter.

All I could think of to say was "Fuck you."

I was hyping and ready to go.

The bell rang, starting round one. Casey came charging out and I circled to my right away from his big round house. I worked back and forth and faked with a right and hit him hard with a left jab, then an overhand right.

"Is that all you got, faggot? My sister hits harder."

Before he could finish I had attacked again with the same fake right-left-right combo.

"Your sister's kicking your ass, b-o-o-y" I returned.

He kicked out with a big round house and missed me completely. I circled to my right immediately after I hit him with the same left-right combo and danced away quickly.

The crowd was going wild with every contact.

Before the fight, Workman and I went for broke on the fight odds and pooled our money and got 2:1 odds and on two bets 3:1 odds. We were about $250 short if I lost, but about $800 up each, if I won.

All through the first round I did the same thing. Circle right and jab hard and come over or under with the right. I didn't get hit once the entire round and was inflicting a major ass-whooping on Carter. I know I wasn't really hurting him physically, but sometimes pride can be beaten worse than the body.

In the second round, Casey was huffing and puffing, so I changed to tactic number two: my Thai boxing technique. I came inside, so his roundhouse couldn't be used, and started pounding his body and legs with power hooks to the side, and knees to the legs. I also used my famous head slam to the chest which infuriated him, because he couldn't stop it and it hurt every time I did it.

When I was in high school, we had a foreign exchange student from Thailand. He was very good at Thai boxing. I taught him wrestling and he taught me Thai boxing. Using your knees, head, and elbows was something I learned very well from him, the hard way. He gave me so many head butts to my chest that I seemed to have a permanent bruise on my chest bone. Man, it hurt when he did it to me. This technique worked great against slower, bigger opponents.

I kept pushing Carter off balance and then power attacking his body. I still hadn't been hit to any affect yet, and he was really huffing and puffing at the end of the second round. Carter must have really been tired because he didn't say anything at the end of the round.

At the beginning of the third round, Casey decided to go for broke. He had been humiliated and beaten and now pride took over his weariness.

"Kill the faggot, kill the faggot, kill the faggot," was repeated over and over again under his breath. He came out steaming. He caught me off guard and rammed a forearm into my chest knocking me back against the ropes and quickly whipped out his famous roundhouse kick, catching me on the shoulder and swinging through to the top of my head. Luckily, it hit my shoulder first or the fight would have been over. I was a bit stunned but not badly. He kicked out again but didn't have enough energy to go high with it and kicked me on the left arm and shoulder. I went across the ring but it didn't hurt much. I had regained my composure and circled right again and started the left-jab-right-hand combo again. I kept this up through the rest of the fight with a constant monologue going while staying out of harms way.

"Looks like the only hurtin' in this fight is my hand on your face there, sissy bo-oy!"

"Should have saved some of that talking energy for fighting."

There was even some spontaneous poetry:
>One punch, two punch, three punch, four.
>Kicking your ass the crowd wants more.
>Five punch, six punch, seven punch, eight.
>Sissy boy's sure making me look great.

Muhammed Ali would have been proud of me.

Casey was near collapse but my poetry sparked him to one last scream and charge. He was swinging wildly but I was able to block and swing around him on the second big right hand. To add humiliation to his last hurrah, I kicked him in the ass as he stumbled by almost sending him over the ropes. Luckily for him, the humiliation ended with the sound of the final bell.

That night all of us went out to celebrate. Casey went out with us for the first time in four months being on the ship. He was very sedate and even friendly to me. Because of the change of nature in him I didn't rub in the victory like I really wanted to.

We were in Gaeta, Italy, about 50 miles north of Naples. It is a nice little port town and has several great small family-owned restaurants. We went to our favorite hole-in-the-wall place run by the Giovanni brothers. They were two fat brothers who spoke pretty good English and were real funny. They could throw a pizza like in old-time Italian restaurants, and they also had fabulous homemade wine.

Casey started drinking wine (it was the first time any of us had ever seen him drink), and after about five or six glasses he spilled his guts out about what was going on in his life.

That afternoon after the fight he received a "Dear John" letter from his wife with divorce papers. She was a devout Christian and had converted him over to her way. But, despite her devoutness she found someone else and just shit-canned him. They had been married about two years.

It was like someone changed the lightbulb in Casey's head. After he finally got all the bullshit out of his system, he started laughing and hollered out "the hell with her," and ordered another bottle of wine. We partied until very early in the morning and Casey finally became one of the guys with a really bad hangover the next day.

Chapter 16

The Extraordinary Jerry West

Jerry West was a Midwest boy from Springfield, Illinois. He was about 5' 7" tall and 155 lbs. He was very patriotic and motivated to join the Navy after he graduated from high school.

Jerry was a great athlete, who played all-conference linebacker and was Illinois state wrestling champ his senior year. He also loved to party hard. Smoking pot and drinking Jack Daniel's, and riding his motorcycle at 100 miles per hour, were just a few of the ways he liked to have fun.

Jerry was one of the lucky ones. He went from boot camp to Hull Technician "A" school right to second class dive school. He didn't have to go through the hassle I did trying to become a diver. He couldn't appreciate how hard it was just to get into diving school from the fleet.

It wasn't that he was mean to me or anything like that. He just didn't show me any respect. I was the same rank and even a little senior to him, but until the day of the wrestling match, I wasn't on the same physical level as far as he was concerned. This meant a lot to him.

A group conversation moved one day to what kind of sports we had played and the subject of wrestling came up.

"So, you wrestled, huh?" Chip Chance asked.

"Ya, I wrestled in high school and college," I answered.

"West was Illinois State Champ and he could kick your ass all over the mat," he provoked.

"Well, a steak dinner says he can't. Put up, or shut up," I countered back.

West, who had been listening to the whole thing, just smiled and said, "Lunchtime on the wrestling mat. Be ready, boy."

When lunchtime came, we arrived in the hanger bay where the wrestling mat was kept. We rolled it out and got ready to wrestle.

It was a really tough match for me because West was strong, aggressive, and very determined. However, he was still not the skill level of a college wrestler like I was. I won 10 to 4 (but also lost because he partially dislocated my shoulder and hurt my knee which both bothered me for several months). Because of this match, I was fully accepted in the dive locker and had a great steak dinner.

Jerry West was an excellent diver and was very good at boat repairs. Besides his diving skills, he had other extraordinary talents. He could snort things up his nose and cough them out his mouth. He especially liked doing this with spaghetti noodles on the mess decks in front of the new sailors. When Sea Hunt was new on board, West sat next to him at lunch when they were serving spaghetti. He got this devilish look on his bearded face and started snorting noodle after noodle up his nose, coughing them into his mouth and chewing them up and eating them. Sea Hunt watched incredulously at what West was doing.

"What the hell are you doing?" he said.

"I love the taste of noodles," West answered.

"Then why the hell are you snorting them up your nose?"

"Jesus, Nelson, don't you know anything? Ninety–five percent of your tastebuds are in your nose, and when I snort the noodles, they taste fantastic," West said, as he took two noodles and snorted one in each nostril.

Sea Hunt couldn't believe what he just saw. We all looked at him and shook our heads in agreement with what West had just said.

"Why don't you try it and see for yourself?" West prodded.

"Have you guys ever done this before?" Sea Hunt asked us.

We all shook our heads in acknowledgment that we had. We also didn't tell him the disastrous results of our trying.

"Go for it, man," I encouraged.

Sea Hunt saw that everyone was watching him now and didn't want to wimp out, so he took a long noodle and started snorting it up his nose. What we didn't tell him was that you needed to lick the noodle or dunk it in water before snorting it, or it would stick in the back of your throat or somewhere in between.

Well, Sea Hunt's noodle made it almost all the way to the back of his throat and then glued itself there. Sea Hunt started gagging and snorting, trying to get the noodle out of his nose. He tried to pull the end which was still hanging from his nose but it snapped off about halfway up his nostril. He was getting desperate, shaking his head back and forth wildly with his mouth opening and shutting like a fish out of water. He thought that maybe the noodle would dislodge itself with these wild movements of panic. We could see the end of the noodle dangling in the back of his throat every time he opened his mouth.

West was grinning the whole time but finally came to Sea Hunt's rescue. He grabbed a glass of milk, shoving it up to Sea Hunt's nose. "Quick, Nelson, snort the milk. It'll get it out!"

In a panic and without thinking Nelson stuck his nose in the milk glass, tipped it up, and snorted deeply. About a quarter of the milk glass went up Sea Hunts nose and down his windpipe along with the noodle. His eyes bulged out and he started coughing and gagging so loudly that everyone on the mess decks stopped and looked. Milk splattered all of us sitting in front of him, but we were laughing too hard to care.

Every time Sea Hunt would cough, we'd start laughing again. He was very embarrassed. While he was coughing he spilled the rest of his milk on his shirt and lap, intensifying the foolish feeling he had for falling for the trick.

In the meantime, West had gone over to the dessert bar and came back with a huge handful of Fig Newton cookies.

Chance leaned over to me and whispered, "Those are West's favorites."

West sat eating cookie after cookie with a strange smile on his face.

"Nelson, I'm sorry I pulled that trick on you. Would you like some Fig Newtons?" West asked nicely.

Nelson was still a little paranoid about the noodle trick and looked around to see if this wasn't another trick, but finally said, "Okay."

West leaned over and barfed a neat pile of milky Fig Newton's on Nelson's tray. Nelson sat there in shock at the puke on his tray. He slowly looked over at West and then at all of us who were grinning at him. He just looked down one more time in disbelief at what was steaming on his tray.

I finally broke the ice. "Hey, are you going to eat those cookies, or just stare at them?"

I then leaned over and stuck my tongue out and pretended to lick a pathway out of the pile of puke. Knowing that West was going to do the barfing routine, I had a cookie already chewed up in my mouth and when I bent down to lick the puke, I put my thumb under my chin and scooped up a pile. Unbeknownst to Nelson, I hid the glop in my hand after I brought my head back up again. The whole movement looked like I just bent over and licked up a scoop of West's regurgitated cookies. I then showed Nelson the chewed-up cookies I had in my mouth by sticking my tongue out, further convincing him. I smacked my lips in contentment and swallowed the mouthful.

"Man, it always tastes better the second time," I said.

Nelson freaked out.

"WHAT! WHAT! AHHH! AHHH! AHHH!" He screamed and picked up the tray and threw it in the air. He jumped up from his seat and did what looked like a backward stuttering moonwalk out of the mess decks.

We were laughing so hard again. My guts still ached from the noodle incident. I looked over at West who was looking at me in a weird way. West's face seemed to say, "you're next."

"If you ever do that to me, I'll kick your ass," I told him with a serious look on my face.

Earlier in the day I had poured some of West's chew spit in his shoe and now he was trying to intimidate me with the threat of being puked on.

West kept looking at me and eating more Fig Newtons. Later, we all left to go back to work. I went to the head, still chuckling about the events at lunch, not thinking anymore about West. After I was done, I went back to the dive locker. When I entered, Chance, Workman, and West were standing around doing nothing. All of a sudden they jumped on me, taking me to the ground. Workman and Chance were holding my arms and West sat on my stomach. He leaned over me and puked Fig Newtons all over my face.

We've all heard of the mother who lifted a car off her child in an emergency and other dramatic feats of strength during very stressful times. This happened to be one of those times for me. My body was electrified. In an amazing feat of strength, I literally threw Workman and Chance off me, as if they were feathers. West was so shocked that he jumped up and ran for the door, but he wasn't fast enough. I caught him.

Three guys were standing just outside the door, when West tried to make his escape. It looked to them like West had been literally sucked back into the dive locker. I grabbed him and threw him almost all the way across the room in the air. He slammed into the bench in front of the aquarium. I leaped in the air with a wild banshee scream, landed right on his chest, and quickly grabbed his shirt under his chin. I twisted tight around his throat and prepared to smash his puking face to hell. Just as I was ready to punch him, Workman and Chance jumped on me again and pulled me off. It gave West just enough time to run for the open door and get lost. I broke loose from them and looked down the passage way to see if I could see him, but he was long gone. Workman and Chance tried to calm me down. They cleaned up the mess. Sea Hunt came in, looked around, and hoped he wasn't going to be the next victim.

"He's gone, but the fucking asshole will pay dearly for this, I guarantee!" I said as if making a sacred oath. There wasn't one person there who didn't believe I'd follow through with my declaration.

Over the next few months, West apologized daily and bought me "mucho" amounts of beer, hoping that I would just forget about the incident in time. At first, I thought of doing something really mean right away, but the longer I took, the more worried West got. Every once in a while, when I knew he was just around the corner, I'd bring up the incident so he'd know I was still planning something. My favorite thing was stand by his bed in the morning and just stare at him as he was waking up with a sinister smile on my face and not say anything. This really jolted him out of restful sleep and really unnerved him. I used the Benunni theory of "just be patient and you'll have your day." In the meantime I was the cat toying with my mouse, and West made a real nice mouse.

Chapter 17

Look Over the Side - Divers Always Get Even

Hull Technician Chief Bret Hinerman was in charge of the Repair 1 division welding shop. He was a good-natured guy who liked to have fun and play jokes on people. He always seemed to be smiling. One of his most favorite things to do was to "fuck with the divers."

The jokes he pulled were always lighthearted and never mean, because that just wasn't his nature. One of his favorite pranks was to call the dive locker and send someone on a fake mission. He was very good at voice imitations and, unless we were looking for it, we were almost always suckered in.

Ring! Ring!

"Dive Locker, Petty Officer Workman. May I help you, sir?" Workman answered in standard Navy protocol.

"Oh, yes, Petty Officer Workman. You're exactly the one I wanted to speak to. This is Dr. Flossmore in Medical and we've had four cases of sexually transmitted diseases up here. One of the men gave us your name because you went out with the same woman as these other four men did. We'd like you to come up here right away so you can be examined. If there's a problem, we can nip it in the bud before it flowers into something more drastic."

Workman fell for it.

"Yes, sir I'll be up there in a few minutes." Workman told Senior Chief Ludwig he was headed for Medical and quickly left.

A few minutes later, a nervous Workman arrived at the Medical Department. He asked for Dr. Flossmore, and he was signaled by the corpsman. He was our personal corpsman pecker checker, the Jewish dick-smith himself, HM 2 Brian Horowitz.

"Workman, go into that room and strip down to your skivvies. The doctor will be there in a while."

What Workman didn't know was that Hinerman had called Horowitz and told him of his plan. Horowitz was always up for a good joke on the divers. Workman undressed down to his shorts and nervously waited for the doctor. He had visions of his cock puffing up and turning colors.

Horowitz came in and said, "Workman, the doc's about to come in. Drop your skivvies put your hands on the table and bend over."

"What the hell for?"

"Because when a dumb ass like you takes one in the ass, he should be in the proper position. By the way, Hinerman says hello, sucker."

Another one of Hinerman's favorite pranks was to call the dive locker several times a day and just hang up when someone came on the line. He called this his diver alert. One morning he was feeling particularly ornery and bored and called the locker 10 times in a row. Everyone knew who it was, and we were tired of answering the phone. When the phone rang for the 11th time, I answered it fully expecting to be hung up on again. When I didn't hear a click right away, I said loudly with great annoyance, "What!"

"Is that how you were taught to answer the phone, sailor? Do you know who this is?" the voice demanded.

I knew exactly who it was. The Executive Officer's voice was very distinctive.

"Do you know who this is?" I returned.

"No."

"Good. Fuck you," and I hung up immediately. Fortunately for me, the phone lines crossed frequently, and the XO thought he'd called the carpenter's shop. He was down there in about 30 seconds to find the caller and ream his ass. In the carpenter shop, the Chief was sitting at his desk shuffling paper when the XO came storming in. After heated words, the Chief told him in no uncertain terms that no one had called the shop for the last half hour. The XO must have dialed a wrong number. Thoroughly exasperated, the XO went back to his office, ready to vent his frustrations out on anyone who got in his way.

Chief Hinerman made daily rounds by the dive locker. He'd stick his head in the door and spout off a new creative line, then slam the door shut. One day Hinerman announced, BOHICA style, "How! No that's not a greeting but a question. How many divers are going to suck my dick today?"

He'd laugh and slam the door. This went on daily. Divers are a patient lot and we knew our time would come one day, but the opportunity arose sooner than we thought.

The fast frigate Cunningham had an emergency pipe welding job. The pipe was connected to the skin of the ship and the cutoff valve attached to it was rusted through and leaking badly. It was ready to collapse. If the pipe gave way, it could cause serious flooding. Even the emergency pipe patch didn't work because the pipe was too far gone. A cofferdam was needed for the outside underwater section of the ship.

A cofferdam is a device that goes over a section of the outer hull of a ship and sucks out the water to allow repairs to be made to the hull from the inside of the ship.

Chief Hinerman had already sent his men over to the Cunningham and went to the dive locker to get things coordinated. Everyone was very professional and quickly got things ready and proceeded to the dive boat with the Chief. The Cunningham was three ships over in the nest next to the Puget Sound.

When Navy ships in foreign ports are in need of repair from the tender-repair ship, they park next to each other in a formation called a nest. The tender is the number one ship hosting up to five ships in the nest. The anchors and chains must be carefully laid to prevent tangling. Before any ship can leave the nest, the divers must go down and swim out the chain to see if it's tangled or not.

Swimming the chain was one of the most dangerous jobs in Naples Harbor. Divers must sit in the middle of the channel while the Italian ferry boat drivers, going to the islands of Capri and Ithaca, are charging in and out of the harbor all day. Whenever we were diving in Naples Harbor, we always had the flare gun loaded and ready to shoot. Italian ferry boat drivers pilot their ships like they drive their cars – pedal to the floor and with no regard for any rules. Harbor speeds are limited to prevent rocking the ships in mooring. Every time a ferry boat went by, it seemed that a new speed record was held. Ferry drivers also loved to play chicken with any boat in the channel – another reason for having the flare gun ready.

One time I was swimming the chain pile at about 90', wearing a Jack Brown Mask, which has no communication system with topside, and I started feeling that my diving harness was being pulled, as I was dragged along the bottom. I heard the engines of a ferry boat above and knew what was happening. Topside, a 200' ferry boat was leaving the harbor and bearing down near our dive boat, deliberately coming closer and closer. Coming into the harbor was another ferry, doing the same thing. It looked like they were on a collision course.

Senior Chief Ludwig shot the first flare into the air to no effect. He then pointed the flare gun directly at the nearest ferry and fired a red phosphorus flare, which bounced off the bridge of the incoming ship and caused it to turn away. Ludwig quickly reloaded, but this time he grabbed the wrong type of flare in his haste.

The second ferry was right on them now. Ludwig pointed the gun at the ferry and let it fly. The ferry turned just in time to miss the back of our dive boat by less then two feet, causing a large wake to really rock the boat. Ludwig's shot accidentally went right through the open door of the bridge and completely smoked out the ferry boat captain. He had to abandon the controls as a tremendous amount of red smoke flowed out of the cabin. He was screaming, coughing, and gesturing his most enthusiastic "fungu you" in our direction, until he noticed where his ship was heading, directly into the rock jetty at the mouth of the harbor. He quickly disappeared into the smoke and the ship turned in time.

The divers were laughing and wondering what the passengers on board the ferry were thinking. Coming back to reality, the divers immediately checked on me. By this time I had my harness off and was getting ready to ditch my gear and surface. I had been given a pretty good ride across the bottom of the harbor.

The Naples Harbor bottom looked like a metal scrapyard with all sorts of dangerously sharp things protruding up at all angles. I was almost impaled a couple of times. I signaled okay and started up. Anytime after that experience, when the dive boat had to go into the channel, which we did every time we drove to work on the nest of ships, we had the flare gun loaded and ready.

With everyone on board, we now headed for the USS Cunningham. Hinerman had the blueprints and was going over the plan. After every break in conversation I'd ask Hinerman, "You can swim, can't you?"

In the background, Hinerman started hearing mutterings from the other divers.

"He's on our turf now."

"You can run, but not very far."

"Twenty-five pounds should take him to the bottom."

He looked over to Senior Chief for some help, but all he got was a "you're-on-your-own" expression.

Hinerman tried to ignore them, but acted apprehensive. We finally pulled up to the bow of the Cunningham and let Workman and Hinerman off the dive boat. Halfway up the bow, Hinerman turned and gave us a big raspberry. Then he ran the rest of the way up to the quarterdeck.

The dive boat pulled up to where the cofferdam was to be placed and moored. The main divers were West and me with the standby diver, Carter. West and I hit the water. The first job was to swim the hogging wire from one side of the ship to the other and pass the end up. Workman, who was topside onboard the Cunningham, led the wire down to us, and we swam it over to the other side. There, Hinerman dropped a rope down to West, who tied it into the eye at the end of the wire. He then signaled Hinerman to haul it up. Hinerman pulled up the wire and secured it to a cleat with a wire strap and shackle. We swam back to the other side of the ship, following the wire as a guide, and signaled Workman that we were done.

During the summer months in Naples Harbor, the water was excessively filthy. There wasn't much tidal change and the harbor resembled a sewer. The visibility in the water was four to five feet on a good day, to zero feet on a bad day, depending if the tide was coming in or going out. One of the concrete sewer pipes, that was suppose to take the city's sewage out of the harbor and dump it a mile out into the Mediterranean Sea, had broken, and raw sewage flowed freely in the harbor. Divers work in some of the most terrible situations and this was the worst condition we had ever encountered. We monitored ourselves constantly for ear infections, boils, skin rashes, and other weird afflictions.

One of the games we played was to see how far we could shoot the numerous condoms that floated in the water. The object was to shoot as many condoms as we could onto the ship we were working on at the time. We enjoyed watching the faces of the sailors as they looked down to find a used rubber on the deck. West liked to blow them up, making various animals. His best creation was a condom poodle. It was proudly displayed as a bow ornament. Making condom animals, and other interesting objects, became the artistic rage among our group, with many unique pieces of art floating around Naples Harbor. Bizarre ideas came out of this: the condom art show, condom mania convention, the book with 101 uses for condoms besides sex, etc.

Another pastime during the slow periods was "turd putting." This was a contest much like shot putting, only we used the feces floating in the harbor. There were stringent rules to these contests and all the divers on the boat acted as judges.

Rule #1: Turds must be at least six inches long.
Rule #2: No hook throwing or flinging.
Rule #3: Turds must stay in one piece or the throw is disqualified.
Rule #4: No swimming into the putt. The diver must be
completely stopped in the water.

With all these rules and restrictions, we were very particular about the turds we chose. They had to be of a certain quality, texture, and composition. It was a highly discussed topic before every contest.

"Yes, the lighter brown and yellow-colored ones don't have as much structural stability as the darker, knotty-looking ones."

"Yes, I agree. You can get much more distance without the disintegration factor and wind gradients influencing the throw." Sometimes scientific analysis was too much and good old common sense had to prevail when it came to turd selection.

"Just give me a constipated man, and I'll win every time," Benunni would say.

The contest began after we picked out our game piece. We would line up at the stern of the dive boat and kick ourselves straight up as high as we could out of the water. In the same fluid motion, we would putt the turd as far as we could. The judges on the boat measured the distance. On windy days they had to be quick, because some of the turds fell apart and went in all directions. Some were even accused of deliberately picking soft ones after dubious measurements by the judges.

That day, there was an outgoing tide and visibility was barely one foot. If West or I were more then three feet underwater, we lost sight of each other so we went down slowly together. I was holding on to West's air hose to stay with him. We found the suction grating and tapped on the hull to make sure we were in the right spot. It was very easy to lose direction under a ship with no visibility and it was very dangerous.

Swimming in the wrong part of the ship could get us pulled into a water intake which had such great suction that it would vacuum all the air out of our mask and lungs. It was one of the great fears of diving on a large ship under no-visibility conditions. Every time a piece of machinery near the ship's skin started up, our hearts would jump in our throats hoping someone wasn't accidentally using the equipment while we were trying to work on it. That had happened already to us, despite big red tags that were placed on the on-off switches. Luckily, no one had been hurt so far.

On the inside of the Cunningham, two of Hinerman's welders were waiting by the pipe to return our signal taps so we knew we were at the correct grating. The oval-shaped suction grate was about three feet long by two feet wide and was covered with a plate with one inch-wide slits spaced evenly down the entire cover. This heavy-duty screen kept large objects from entering the pump and system.

West tapped on the hull and heard the return taps. He took his knife and scratched a line on the bottom of the ship as we returned to the dive boat. We scratched this line so that on the way back to the suction grating we wouldn't get lost.

Topside, Senior Chief Ludwig and Mike "Sea Hunt" Nelson had extra weights on the cofferdam so we could drag it underwater. The rubber on the edges and on the inside of the cofferdam made it buoyant so it would float up against the bottom of the ship when it was placed there. Without the weights on it, we couldn't pull it down under the ship. Once the cofferdam was in place, the weights were cut loose and pulled back to the diving boat. The cofferdam was lowered over the side and passed to us. West and I each grabbed the handles that were welded on the sides of the aluminum box and swam it over, looking for our scratch mark. We found it and started down.

Once we were under the bottom of the Cunningham and had the cofferdam in place, we cut the weights loose. Using a precut piece of string, we stretched it out from the center of the suction grating and marked the dimensions on the bottom of the ship. That way we knew when the cofferdam was centered over the grating. We then swam around a bit and found the hogging line and centered it right next to the eductor. Satisfied with the setting, we swam back to the dive boat. Upon surfacing, we signaled Workman to tighten the hogging wire with the come-a-long hoist and turned the water on for the eductor.

West and I surfaced and waited temporarily for Workman to do his part. Hinerman decided to hawk major spit luggies on us below. I looked up when Hinerman called to me, and then he'd hawk a good one on my face plate. Even in the wind and 20' up on the ship, Hinerman was amazingly accurate.

"God, I want to get him," I bellowed to West, after another direct hit nailed me on the top of the head.

Just then an amazing sight came into view. Off in the distance, I saw the largest one-piece turd I had ever seen in all my time in the Naples Harbor. My eyes widened as the 18" long, 2" in diameter monster turd floated towards me.

This was a turd that could qualify someone for the Olympics. I fantasized receiving the gold medal and setting a new world's record for turd putting. When that delusion passed, a better and more immediate thought entered my mind.

Slowly, and with great care, I paddled the water so it would float right up to me. "Come home to daddy." I could not image the size of the human being or the butt hole that produced this monster and hoped I'd never meet him or her in any Naples bar. Once it was mine, I twisted it in a corkscrew pile, keeping it firmly in one piece. I signaled Workman who looked over the side, wide-eyed at the size of the turd in my hand. He read my mind instantly. Workman called over to Hinerman and said the divers needed him. Workman held his hand over the side to mark the spot so I could aim from down below.

"Hey, they need something down there," Workman yelled, guiding Hinerman to the right place. "Down here." Hinerman leaned over the side and looked down.

Workman signaled me by opening his fist. I sprung into action. Kicking as hard as I could, I raised out of the water nearly to my waist and flung the giant turd toward the inquiring face of Hinerman. It all happened in slow motion. The monster turd hurled upwards at tremendous speed. Hinerman's eyes bulged out of their sockets as he saw the mammoth turd uncurl in mid air, achieving its full and glorious length. Shooting through the air, its size was magnified even more. As it rapidly moved toward Hinerman's face, he instinctively froze. As the monster turd reached the apex of its flight, a large gust of wind pushed it towards Hinerman's nose, where it deposited a respectable chunk on the tip.

There stood Hinerman in shock, cross-eyed, and looking at the brown poop on the end of his nose. The divers on the boat died with laughter. Hinerman was beside himself, repulsed – sickened and not knowing what to do. He instinctively tried to wipe it off with his hand, but didn't want to touch the pasted turd pile. He looked to Workman for help, but he was doing an Irish jig as he exploded with laughter. Hinerman looked around helplessly as the fecal chunk stubbornly clung to his nose. All the divers had tears running down their faces. Hinerman finally ran to the chief's quarters on the Cunningham.

West and I didn't get a chance to see what went on up on the dive boat because what goes up, must come down. And looking up, we saw what appeared to be a large wooden piling coming down at us, and we reacted quickly, diving to safety underwater before the monster turd could hit us.

Later, it was reported that when the turd hit the water, it nearly capsized the dive boat, and the water pressure from the impact shoved West and me deep into the mud at the bottom of the harbor. An aircraft carrier moored two piers over, was rocked violently. At least, that's how the story went.

Our payback slowed Hinerman down for a little while. One thing could be said for him: he was resilient. It didn't take long before Chief Brown-noser Hinerman was back to his old tricks, though. Whenever we'd go through the welding shop the banter would start.

"Do you smell shit?" West asked loudly.

"Why, yes I do. What could it be?"

"Let's ask the Chief. He "nose" where it's coming from."

And speaking directly to the Chief, I said "What I want to know is how you could tan only the tip of your nose."

"What I want to know is how you're able to carry your entire brain on the tip of your nose?"

"Next time, Chief, I'll wipe better, okay?"

The Chief took it in stride. He'd just slowly scratch his nose and smile secretively. He'd get even.

Chapter 18

"Dickbreath" Wenckel and the Turd Chasers

Every night there was a movie for the crew. Some of the movies were good, some were terrible. Some had titties, and they were great. The most favorite movie was Amazon Queen, and it was never allowed to leave the ship to go into fleet rotation. Other movies would be traded from ship to ship in port with the new movies always coming from ships new to the rotation in the Mediterranean. But not Amazon Queen.

At 1930 hours the crew started gathering on the mess decks to secure their seats for the 2000 hours show. It was always the typical seating arrangements divided by division or race. Blacks sat to the left of the screen, the Filipinos sat in the back right. The divers and hull technicians sat front center and the Mexicans and Puerto Ricans sat behind us. Anyone else took what was left. The table with divers and Hull Techs was full very early and people were playing cards and bullshitting with one another to pass the time until the movie started. The mess decks were going to be packed this night because Amazon Queen was the feature.

About once every two weeks this movie was played. It was about a topless tribe of Amazon women warriors who raided nearby villages for men and used them as sex slaves. When they served their purpose, the men were then used as work slaves until they died. The favorite scene was the battle for the new queen, after the old queen died.

After many elimination trails only two Amazon warriors remained. The evil, large-breasted brunette battled the good, large-breasted blonde in an oiled wrestling match. The winner of the match was the new Queen of the Amazons. The crew would go wild during the match and many times it was run backwards and forwards again and again to get the full impact of the spectacle. We had seen the movie so many times that all of us knew the dialogue, and hundreds of sailors would talk along with the characters. It would sound like liturgical responses at a Catholic mass.

That evening, I happened to sit across the table from HT-1 Willy Wenckel. He was my shop supervisor in the ship's company "R" Hull

Technician Division before I went to diving school. Wenckel looked just like Fred Flintstone, the cartoon character.

"Hey, Willy, how's it going?" I ask.

"Why the fuck do you ask? You don't give a shit anyway," snapped Wenckel.

"Oh, Willy, you hurt my feelings. I truly miss unplugging shitters and working side by side with a true sewage professional like yourself," I professed mockingly. I looked closely at Wenckel's head and pointed at something, "Hey, what's that in your hair?"

"Fuck you. I know it was you. You were the one, you fucking asshole."

I looked at him in mock disbelief, pretending to be offended at his accusation. My guilty smirk would admit to nothing.

When I was first on board the Puget Sound, I worked in R division, which is in the ship's engineering department. We took care of all the repairs of our ship. I worked in the 3-M maintenance shop under the supervision of HT-1 Willy Wenckel. Our responsibility was to supervise all the other divisions to maintain the ship's firefighting equipment such as portable fire extinguishers and hose stations. Hull Technician's were known as "turd chasers", because plumbing was one of the unsavory jobs assigned. When plumbing emergencies hit, we had to go on shitter patrol to unplug the ship's sewage piping.

It seemed like the sewage system was always a problem. Disgruntled sailors flushed all sorts of things down the toilets like clothing, mop heads, whole rolls of toilet paper, and – worst of all – plastic bags. We hated when this happened. To get the pipes unplugged, the clean-out cap had to be removed which usually spewed out nasty sewage all over the deck. Then, a rotor-router machine, with a clean-out wire, would be sent down the piping to clear out the clog. Sometimes it took a few minutes and sometimes it took hours.

On one occasion, we spent several hours trying to unclog the main sewage drain system. We finally narrowed it down to a large 6" pipe located in the engineering berthing area. Because this particular system affected three quarters of the ship's bathrooms, including the Captain's, getting it unclogged quickly was a high priority. We took off the clean-out cap and expected a ton of sewage to flow out. Instead, only a very small amount dribbled forth. Within arm's length of the clean out cap was a thick plastic bag hooked up in the pipe corner coupling. The only way to relieve the pressure was to poke a hole in the bag and let the sewage flow out.

There was probably 200 gallons of sewage backed up in the pipe, pushing to get through the clog. All of us on shit patrol drew straws to see who was going to reach in there and poke the bag. I lost. There were close to 150 grinning idiots standing all around me in the engineering berthing area, watching to see when I got shit blasted. I had to endure all the stupid comments from the engineering crowd.

"Putting his hand in shit is better then feeling pussy to a Hull Tech."

"He's just going to get some chocolate frosting for the Hull Tech cake."

"That's how a turd chasing Hull Tech takes a really good shower."

"I shit, shower, and shave before I go in to town. Hull Techs' got it all backwards. They shit-shower and shave. Then they wonder why they don't get women."

I gallantly walked up to the pipe opening with a knife in my hand and reached in. I closed my eyes tightly expecting the worst to gush in my face. My arm went in deeper and deeper until I felt the plastic bag with my knife and rammed it, instantly jerking my arm out of the way of the backed-up sewage that immediately shot out like a fire hose under high pressure. It shot right past me and bounced off the nearby lockers, ricocheting all over the laughing spectators. I slammed the cap back on the clean-out fitting and screwed it on tightly. Shit and toilet paper were everywhere and on everyone. Because I had jumped back in time, I was the only one not doused with it. There was only one smile left and I was wearing it.

"Looks like all you engineering, turd chasing wanna-bes are ready to go to town," I announced proudly.

After that experience, we were determined to find a better way to solve piping clogs so that it wouldn't result in such a time-consuming and messy procedure. We put our heads together and came up with a solution. All the main drain pipes were drilled and quick-connected with one-way fittings. We had hard rubber plugs with T handles manufactured to fit in the toilets so the water couldn't back up through the toilets from the pressure about to be released in the piping. When all the plugs were installed and a valve up stream in the piping from the blockage was closed, a CO_2-filled fire extinguisher with 1,800 psi was hooked up to the piping quick connect. The cold CO_2 at 1,800 psi was shot into the piping and when it hit the warmer atmosphere and expanded, it super pressurized the piping and blew out the clog. The only negative was if there were any weaknesses in the piping system, it would blow the pipes apart. Also, if any of the toilet plugs weren't set securely, a serious flying missile could emerge. But, our creative solution more than made up for the very infrequent problems that could happen. Still, great care was taken to not shoot too much CO_2 into the piping.

Every morning after quarters and daily shop job assignments were given, HT-1 Wenckel would retire to the head for at least one hour every day to do his morning constitution. He would go to the same stall in the engineering berthing head and read fuck books, and then sleep. Usually about an hour later, he'd wake up, finish his business, and go back to work. After months of this, and being more then his usual jerky self to everyone, the shop decided to get even. Plans were made and the equipment was gathered. "Operation Fat Willy" was ready to go.

The next morning after job assignments were given, everyone went off to work. Wenckel, like clockwork, went for his morning constitution. As soon as he left the shop, everyone mustered back again in the shop to implement the plan.

First, we checked to see if Wenckel was settled in. Second, an "Out of Order" sign was put on the door of the head. No one ever crossed that boundary if they'd ever seen a sewage back up. Third, plugs were put into the two toilets down line from Wenckel's and CO_2 was connected to the drain pipe quick-connect fitting. Fourth, a valve down line was closed to isolate the system that connected the toilets he was sitting on. Everyone was set and patiently waited the appropriate time to execute.

After about 10 minutes, we got tired of hearing Wenckel's loud breathing and pushed the mission along by slamming one of the stall doors and flushing the urinals a couple of times. This stirred Willy and he started to unroll the toilet paper.

"Hold on," I signaled with a closed fist.

After the second time the toilet paper was unraveled, the engage signal was given. The CO_2 bottle blasted just as Wenckel flushed the toilet. Sewage water blasted up and out of the toilet, lifting Wenckel right off the seat into the air. Water and sewage chunks shot out the side and hit the ceiling. By the time Wenckel quit screaming, the plugs were pulled, the CO_2 was disconnected, the "Out of Order" sign was taken down, the isolation valve was opened, and everyone boogied back to the shop with everything put away neatly. We were quietly doing paperwork when Wenckel stormed through the door. Putrid water dripped from his hair and brown streaks were on his pants and shirt.

"What happened to you?" HTFN Pena asked straightfaced with concern. "Are we having a flood somewhere?"

"I know you fucking guys did it!" he yelled.

"Did what?" I replied. "I just got back from the machine shop."

Everyone looked concerned. Wenckel scanned each sailor for a telltale sign of guilt. Everyone kept true to the game and Wenckel had no alternative but to go shower and change his clothes. As he left I said, "Hey, Willy." I pointed to something pasted on his head. Wenckel reached up and pulled off a big chunk of brown stained toilet paper from his hair. Totally pissed, he stormed off for the showers.

From then on, every time I'd see HT-1 Willy Wenckel, I'd always stare at his hair, pointing at an imaginary thing attached to it. Wenckel could never get anyone to admit involvement. He was just a big bag of hot air, but he didn't sleep easy on the toilet anymore and he changed stalls on a daily basis.

So now, sitting across from me on the mess decks, waiting for the movie to begin, was Willie Wenckel. A messenger approached him and announced that he had a phone call from Damage Control Central. Willy got up and went, but unfortunately left his coffee cup on the table.

"Hey, let's dick wipe Willy's cup," one of the Hull Techs urged.

"Ya-a-a-a!" everyone at the table shouted.

Wenckel's cup was passed around the table as each guy wiped their penis around the rim. After the cup went to each of the 11 guys, it was set back exactly in its place. A few seconds later, Wenckel came back and sat down.

I said, "You know, Willy, every guy at this table dick wiped your cup."

Wilson gave me a "ya, right," look and picked up his cup, and in a very exaggerated way, stuck out his tongue and slowly licked the entire rim. He looked back at me with a smug expression on his face.

I smiled at him and said, "Did it taste good, Willy?"

Then, all 11 of us stood up, displaying our exposed penises to Wenckel. The laughter was loud, as 500 sailors joined in the fun. Wenckel looked at all the cocks on display and yelled, "You fuckers," and threw his coffee on as many of us as he could and stalked away, to the calls of a new name.

Thus, the saga of Willy Dickbreath Wenckel began. The man who could lick 11 cocks at once. With a warm-up act like that, Amazon Queen was better than ever that night.

Chapter 19

Radiation Man

ET 1 William P. Elliot, III, was new on board the Puget Sound, and worked in the R-6 Division or Radiation Control shop. All the members of the shop were nuclear qualified. Elliot came from a well-to-do family and his father had owned a successful chemical testing company. At least that's what Elliot wanted everyone to think. They had a big house, a nice new car, and they went on great vacations. The only problem was his father spent his money as fast as he earned it and unfortunately died in a car accident leaving his family in incredible debt.

The family then discovered after his untimely death that he left no life insurance and very high business debt. William's mother knew nothing about finances because her husband took care of everything. The money that they did have ran out very quickly, and she was left with no alternative but to liquidate their assets.

Elliot was entering his junior year in college at USC when this tragedy struck. College was put on hold and an alternative plan was made. The Navy college plan went into effect. Elliot didn't want to be just another sailor, so he chose the nuclear program because only the intellectually elite qualified, or so his recruiter had said. "Yes, that's me, intellectually elite," he boasted later.

Nuke school was easy for Elliot and he finished Number One in his class. For his first assignment, he was given orders to report to the USS Queenfish, a fast attack submarine docked at Pearl Harbor, Hawaii. But Elliot wasn't in Hawaii for long, because the submarine crew was split into two groups, Blue and Red. While one crew patrolled, the other stayed in port and trained. Elliott was assigned Blue crew and he went on patrol two weeks after his arrival.

Elliott was happy about going down. He'd done a test run at sub school and everything went fine, but going down for 90 to 105 days without surfacing was something completely different. After about a week under, Elliott was unable to sleep. Everything was closing in on him and he became short tempered and very irritable. Even though he was doing an excellent job running the plant in engineering, he was a real jerk. There were so many complaints about him that the Chief had to talk to him.

"Hey, what's up, Elliot?" asked Chief Piser.

"What do you mean?"

"Well, you're acting like some chick two weeks late for her monthly."

William proceeded to tell the chief that he felt he was losing it and was having a hard time controlling himself. Piser understood. He'd been in the submarine Navy for 14 years and had seen several sailors go through this adjustment period. He also knew that some never adjusted. More than once, he had seen sailors go completely loony and have to be restrained and sedated until they were dropped off somewhere.

Elliot checked in to see the Doc, as the chief suggested. Despite all the help and encouragement from the crew, Elliott was getting worse. During one of the watches in engineering, he exploded. His relief was about five minutes late and Elliot came unglued and had to be restrained. He was taken to sickbay screaming until he was sedated. Five days later, he was dropped off in Guam at the medical facility.

Elliot was then assigned shore duty at the repair facility at the Submarine Base in Pearl Harbor. He calibrated, repaired, and installed radiation detection devices and was also on the emergency spill team for radiation accidents. Life was easy. He made E-6, First Class Petty Officer, his first time up, and received his next set of orders: sea duty USS Puget Sound where he'd be patrolling the Mediterranean sea.

I met Elliot for the first time about three weeks after he had checked on board the Puget Sound.

"Hey, what's your name?" I asked, trying to be friendly.

"Petty Officer Elliot," he answered like an arrogant snot.

"Okay, Elliot, I'm here to pick up our dosimeters." These were devices that measured exposure to radiation and they have to be worn by divers working on nuclear submarines or ships.

"That's Petty Officer Elliot to you, or you won't get anything out of this shop unless you show proper respect," he replied arrogantly.

Confused by his immediate hostility, I decided to slap some sense into him and started to walk behind the counter where the asshole stood.

"I'll teach you a little lesson about respect, you little radiac nerd."

The chief who had great respect for the divers jumped in quickly to divert a messy situation. He'd seen what divers could do to people that pissed them off and didn't want anything to happen to his new guy.

"Hold on," the chief demanded. "Elliot, go get those dosimeters for him now."

Elliot gave a hard look at the chief and angrily picked up a bag of the devices and set them on the counter in front of me. He had an evil look on his face.

I took the bag and said, "You're lucky this time, geek."

After I left, the chief went up to Elliot." What the hell were you trying to do," the Chief asked "get your ass kicked?"

"Divers are a bunch of stupid assholes. That son-of-a-bitch was disrespectful to me."

"Look, son, you're going to have to get rid of that Radcon elite attitude right now. You're not on shore duty anymore. The divers are the captain's darlings and they get whatever they want. You'll also be working with them when they work on the nuke cruisers as a Radcon monitor, so walk lightly – or you'll be in for a lot of problems."

The reason Elliot hated divers so much dated back to Pearl Harbor Subbase. The SCUBA and second class diving school was right across the street from the Radcon barge where he worked. Every morning the divers would run by chanting their songs in formation. They were in-shape, well-muscled guys, which was the antithesis of Elliot who stood 5' 6" and weighed 125 lbs.

Elliot had met a female sailor working on the base and got up the nerve to ask her out. She was pretty and fun to talk to. Elliot had a big crush on her. He dated her twice and thought everything was going fine until he saw her one afternoon with a diver at the Beaman Center Enlisted Club.

The girl signaled for Elliott to come over. "Elliot, I'd like you to meet my boyfriend, Todd."

"Hey, Elliot, thanks for watching after my girl while I was on leave," Todd said with the look and air of someone who had no worry of being threatened by the likes of Elliot. Todd smiled at Elliot in an arrogant sort of way, and walked away, hand in hand with Sharon. Elliot was publicly humiliated and hated divers after that.

Seeing me walk into his shop brought back all the animosity and feelings of inferiority that divers brought out in him.

Finally, after several weeks, it was Elliot's turn to go to the dive boat and be the radiation monitor while the divers worked on the nuclear cruiser USS California. He tried to get other people to go in his place, even offering cash, but the Chief wouldn't allow it.

"You're going to have to go and learn this stuff whether you want to or not. Jesus, Elliot, get over it. And please don't make an ass out of yourself or you'll be accidentally knocked off the boat. Isn't that right, Hernandez?" the Chief asked.

Hernandez smiled and said, "Yeah, they all looked concerned after I was in the water, but I know they were laughing behind my back. I mean there were turds and everything in the water. God, I don't see how those guys do that. Remember if they ask if you can swim, watch out."

After I realized what a dickhead we were dealing with, the divers got together to hatch a plan to teach Elliott better manners. We needed to get everything we could on Elliot to know just how far we could push him, so West and I went to the personnel office and convinced a friend to show us Elliot's record. This was against all the rules of privacy, but because the petty officer had been bribed with a K-bar combat knife and two green hats, access to any personnel record was open to us. This included any disciplinary action, school grades, and other personal information. We also did the same thing in the medical department where we consulted our buddy, Brian Horowitz, our Pecker Checker Corpsman extraordinaire. The medical records revealed many interesting tidbits about Elliot's mental state and all this information was used to set up a little charade. One of the pieces of info in the psych evaluation was a direct quote from Elliot, "don't call me Billy!" Now we had a new name.

West saw Elliott leave the quarterdeck from the fantail and he ran into the R-6 shop.

"Hey, Hernandez, have you got a pegged-out dosimeter? One that's top-ended out?"

"Yeah, what do you need that for?"

West just gave his devilish smile.

"I don't want to ask," laughed Hernandez.

"Thanks, see ya later." West smiled after he received the broken dosimeter that was stuck reading a super-high radiation reading.

As in any good acting job, rehearsals are the key to a good performance. Nelson had previously gone to the R-6 shop and borrowed a radiac on the premise that, he was conducting training on radiation detection and monitoring devices. Because all the divers were nuclear worker qualified, this made sense to the R-6 guys who were more than happy to let the divers do their own training. After testing the meter on different settings and at different distances, it was discovered that the second to the highest sensitivity top ended the meter without totally pegging it out. The high-level light would come on and a high whirring sound would distinguish a high reading.

Down on the boat, everything was set. The diving hats were ready and the divers were, too. Workman was primary diver and I was standby. All the divers wore luminescent diving watches which had a radioactive charge. They were banned by the Navy, but all the divers wore them anyway because they were the only watches that glowed even in the filthiest water. If a radiac was on high-end sensitivity and passed over the watch, the meter would peg it out and sound an alarm.

We also used night glow sticks. They were plastic tubes with a small glass tube inside. When this tube was crushed, two chemicals mixed causing a glowing light that lasted anywhere from eight to 12 hours. The colors could be white, purple, red, yellow/green, or orange. This day we picked yellow-green.

The thought of having to go out alone on the dive boat with those asshole divers on the water turned Elliott's anger into worry. He would be at their mercy out there. Well, he'd just hang on tight to the $10,000 Radiac and they wouldn't dare throw him in with that piece of expensive equipment.

The crew was all aboard including a very nervous Elliot. Everybody was professional and courteous to him. "It must be that Senior Chief is on board and those guys are staying in line," thought Elliott. Now his confidence and arrogance returned. "They won't touch me now."

The boat pulled away with Senior Chief driving. He loved to drive, so when he was aboard, everyone knew who was driving. The boat first pulled up to the USS Ingles, a fast frigate. Because this was a non-nuclear ship, Elliot had nothing to do but watch. He had to admit that the divers knew what they were doing. While reviewing the ship's blueprints, they asked many technical questions of which Elliot had no idea what they were talking about. It seemed like a different language – suction gradients, fairweathers, bilge keels. He was actually starting to have some respect for diver intelligence.

After the USS Ingles inspection was completed, the divers were off to the nuclear cruiser USS California. By the time the diving boat moored next to the California, Workman was ready to hit the water. He had his dosimeter attached to his leg pocket. Unbeknownst to Elliot, Workman also had the pegged-out dosimeter in his other leg pocket and the glow stick was tucked inside his wetsuit top.

The job on the California was a full hull inspection involving several dives and underwater video camera work. Workman started aft on the starboard and worked his way around the ship. As the boat was required to move, the diver was brought out of the water for radiation inspection. Elliot performed the task of sweeping over Workman's body with his Radiac meter to see if he received any radiation while diving near a certain part of the ship. He dutifully marked off each section of the ship on his chart and recorded zero readings. Workman made sure that the meter never got near his watch. He'd watch Elliot and plotted the best time to execute the plan.

Workman finished inspecting the last section of the California and before he arrived at the ladder of the dive boat, he had changed out the operational dosimeter to the one that was stuck on a high reading. While he was sitting on the bottom step of the ladder, he handed up the video UDATS system, and took off his diving hat. In the meantime, the Senior Chief, who was also part of the setup, distracted Elliot from watching Workman.

"Hey, Petty Officer Elliot, how do you check if the calibration is still correct after being out there all day long?"

Elliot was in the spotlight and fell hook, line, and sinker for the ploy. He went into a lengthy lesson of calibration techniques and checks. In the meantime, Workman had unzipped his wetsuit top and broken the glow stick inner tube. The two chemicals mixed and started glowing. He cut the tube top off, pouring the glowing contents all over his chest. He quickly zipped up his wet suit to cover himself up. He then climbed up to the deck of the dive boat. The Senior Chief motioned to Elliot that Workman was now ready to be monitored.

Workman handed Elliot the pegged-out dosimeter with a very distressed look on his face as he winced and started coughing violently. Elliot checked the dosimeter and looked shocked. Workman coughed even more, almost gagging as Elliot quickly took his meter and ran his sensor over the complete length of Workman. Every time he went over Workman's chest, he got extremely high readings. Workman started to turn bright red and gagged even more.

Elliot was starting to panic. He flipped to the next highest level and quickly ran the sensor over Workman's body again. Workman was now at an Academy Award-level of performance. At the exact time that Elliot swept across his chest for the final time, Workman stuck his watch right in front of the sensor, pegging out the meter and setting off the high-level alarm. At this moment he pulled open his wet suit, exposing the yellow-green glow of his chest as he fell on the deck in a full grand mall seizure, complete with foam dripping from his mouth and a tightly clenched jaw. Workman was flopping around with horrible gurgling sounds coming from his mouth, rolling back his eyes so only the whites showed.

When Elliot saw his eyes like this, he screamed, "He's radioactive!!"

Elliot whirled around and everyone had disappeared. "Hey! Where...?" Elliott was totally freaking out, yelling, "HELP, HELP!" He turned to run to the hatch and collided with a rack of diving hoses that hit him right in the nuts. In the meantime, Workman had "died" with one last shrieking spasm, and green radioactive slime glowing on his chest.

Elliot was in total panic, screaming and jumping up and down but he made it into the hatch, frantically negotiating the steps into the compartment. There he saw five giant, cheesy, shameless grins. "You're crazy," he screamed, unable to figure out just had happened. Maybe he was hallucinating.

Finally, the dead Workman, who had wiped some of the glow stick on his face, around his eyes, and in his mouth, rose from the dead and started walking towards Elliott, zombie-like, drooling the glowing green spit. Elliot screamed again and bolted up the stairs and ran for the ladder on the pier piling. In his panic, he missed the first step and fell into the water. Looking up at the boat he saw six laughing faces staring down at him. It finally struck him what had happened. He slowly swam to the back of the boat.

   After Elliott was pulled back on board he sat silently as the dive boat returned to the Puget Sound. He instantly departed and tried to hide and stay out of sight. But wherever Elliott was seen, walking anywhere, someone would yell out, "Hey! Look over there! It's Billy the Radiation Man." And thus, he was known for the next three years on board the USS Puget Sound, as "Billy the Radiation Man." This incident only reinstated the warning throughout the ship that no one ever messed with divers!

Chapter 20

Rolling Home

The cruise was over. Looking back over our whole adventure, the work never seemed to end, and the days were a kind of blur from morning to night. But now, as we were headed back home to the States, those days seemed to have gone by in a flash.

We left Rota, Spain, and passed the ball to the USS Hundley, the repair tender taking our place. Everyone was very excited about going home, except for me. I didn't have anybody waiting for me back there, and I had more fun in the Mediterranean than I ever did in the squid-hating town of Norfolk, Virginia. I could have stayed on for another cruise.

We pulled into the Atlantic and the seas got bigger and bigger. It wasn't rough, but huge rollers were regularly moving by us. I knew the seas were going to get pretty big, but I didn't expect what actually happened.

When I was at the beach in Rota, I surfed some pretty big waves and had a great time. I stashed one of my boards in the back room of the dive locker and had several occasions to go surfing over the last six months. From the swells that hit Rota, I knew it was going to be big in the open Atlantic.

The swells got bigger and bigger. Our ship was nearly 900' long but it felt like it was a toy boat in a bath tub. On the third day out, the swells increased, and we got 40 to 50' giant rollers. Up on the bridge, which was about 70' above the water, huge mountains of ocean could be seen coming from the north. The weather report told of an Arctic storm blasting our way with seas over 100'.

Before we left Rota, we had repaired and painted our dive boat, and it was ready to go. All our dive gear was maintenanced and put away, so the only thing we did was hang around the dive locker, read, and work out. It was boring, but to do anything else was dangerous with the ship rocking and rolling so much. The objective was to not get hurt, because it was easy to be thrown off balance and impale yourself on equipment. Several guys had already gotten hurt when the ship rose and fell.

The Senior Chief did us a great favor during the cruise by convincing our division officer, Lt. Roberts, who was also a diver, that we shouldn't be on the regular watch bill and should have our own watch bill as duty divers. This worked out great because Senior Chief and Carter rarely went anywhere, so they would take the duty diver watch almost all the time, leaving the rest of us free.

Standing watch is probably the single-worst thing required of a military person. In most cases, it's four to eight hours of standing around bored everyday at sea, and every three days while in port. The hardest part of standing watch is having to work all day and get up in the middle of the night, stand around, stay awake, and do almost nothing. It throws all your sleep patterns off, and makes a lot of really grumpy sailors walking around the ship.

Our job as duty divers was to clear the debris that got caught in the small boat engine water suction screens. This only happened in Naples, and most of the time it was an accumulation of condoms that got sucked into the intake screen. Our job was to free-dive and clear the intake. This was standard duty except for that infamous time in Naples.

A barge with more than 10,000 chickens sank in Naples Harbor and there were chicken bodies floating around everywhere. For about three days, we were constantly clearing the water suction screens. At night, it was really scary. Because of the dead foul, every wharf rat in Italy came down to the harbor to dine on fresh chicken meat. These rats were huge, with bodies as big as lap dogs. Just before dusk, they would come out of their hiding places along the rock jetty by the thousands and silently slide into the water. They were really hard to see in the night water except for their fierce, red eyes. Sometimes I would swim right into them and they would jump and try to attack me. With little, beady, glowing, red eyes and large yellow fangs, they'd squirm around and hiss as I shined my underwater flashlight on them. Talk about scaring the living shit out of you.

On several night dives I had to stab at the ugly mothers just to get them to back off. Rats are not full-time water animals and are at a disadvantage while swimming, thank God. I would not want to meet a bunch of them on shore.

We were really glad when a storm came in and flushed the harbor clean of all the chicken carcasses. But even diving among huge fighting rats was worth it, if it meant not standing an eight-hour duty every three days. So, relieved of duty watch, all we did was read and watch the swells. It hypnotized us. Feeling the power of the ocean was so exhilarating and humbling – and we were out in the middle of it all.

There were three different levels of open fantail on our ship. The lowest was about 30' above the water. My old hull technician shop was located back there. It was fun to stand at the very back end of the ship and watch the water rise above us. Right when it was about to come over the edge of the short bulk head, we would suddenly lift up to see nothing but sky. Then we'd drop back down to do it all over again. The water mountain was so close that we were able to reach out and stick our arms into it as it came by. At night, no one was allowed on the fantail or open decks except those standing fantail watch.

During the fifth night out, really big swells started to roll in. The skies were very clear with a full moon. If you knew the person on watch, you could sneak outside and see the night beauty of the moon reflected on the ocean. On this particular night, Electricians Mate Third Class Lacey was on watch. He was a black guy from Philadelphia, about 6', 190 lbs. I knew him well from our boxing and wrestling teams. Lacey was also in the engineering department with me when I was in the hull technician's shop.

Lacey was deathly afraid of being washed over the side in the middle of the night. He told me that standing the fantail watch alone at night was the scariest thing he'd ever done in his life. Now, we're talking about a guy who grew up in a rough ghetto of Philly.

"Come on, Lacey, let's go out to the fantail and really see the waves," I egged him on.

"No way, man! With my luck, we'd both get washed over, and you, being a diver and all, would live, and I'd be shark food."

Two of my HT buddies came through the water-tight door out to the fantail and said hello to Lacey.

"Hey, guys, big bad Lacey's pussing out. The ball-less motherfucker won't go out to the end and do the nut check, and stick his hand in the water. He's afraid he'll get washed over. Let's show him how real men do it."

My two buddies and I walked out to the end of the fantail and looked out. It was a rush watching the water rise and sink, only inches from us. We stuck out our arms to touch the water as we rose up and down. We showed Lacey that there was nothing to it. I knew what we were doing wasn't the smartest or safest thing, but it sure was a rush. After about five minutes of doing this we walked back to the large anchor windless where Lacey was hiding and continued to ridicule his manhood.

"Jesus, Lacey, if you had just one inch of dick, you'd walk out there and stick your arm in it once." Lacey still wouldn't budge, looking petrified at the rising and falling sea.

"God, no wonder the ricionis in Naples loved you. Now we know who the big black limp one was. We heard them talking. I guess all that tough guy stuff from Philly was a bunch of crap. Jesus Lacey, you're a wuss. Just walk out there and stick it in once, like a real man."

Finally Lacey gave in. It was the real man thing that finally got to him. Now, Lacey was wearing a sound-powered, telephone headset that all the fantail watches had to wear. He slowly walked out, dragging his phone cord in back of him like a life line. About half way out he looked back.

"Come on, go for it!" HT-3 Schneider yelled at him.

Lacey turned towards the fantail and carefully walked the rest of the way. He looked back again with tension and fear written all over his face. He waited for the water to come up and held on to the edge of the waist-high bulkhead, and stuck his arm in up to the elbow. He turned and looked back at us like he had just exorcised a demon. He stuck his arm in the water again. When he looked back again he was like a little kid having the time of his life. Lacey stuck his arm in the water again and again as the powerful sea rose and fell.

Everything was going wonderfully for Lacey until we felt a sudden roller-coaster drop and then the ship caught us as we started back up. In a split second, fun and exhilaration turned to fear as Lacey was thrown forward against a pole that held up the overhead deck above. Just as quickly, Lacey was next thrown aft against the short bulkhead, almost going over the side. A solid wall of water from the overhead to the top of the bulkhead blasted in and over him.

The giant wave carried Lacey almost to the back of the fantail. The waves crashed as the ship heaved up and the next swell sucked all the water back out again. Lacey was dragged back towards the stern and the open ocean. He started screaming and flailing his arms and legs.

Despite the danger of it, watching Lacey scrambling for a hand hold was the funniest thing you could imagine. I'd never seen eyes that wide with terror since Sea Hunt's first solo dive.

Lacey finally got a tight hold until the water went back out. Lacey was up on his feet running towards us like a mad man. He looked like one of those cartoon characters that jump up and take running steps in the air with the bongo drums wailing before they hit the floor and finally get moving. Lacey's only problem was that he forgot he had on his sound-powered phone headset. As he ran full speed toward us, the cord ran out and yanked the phone under his chin, snapping his head back like a slingshot. His feet flew out from under him as he became airborne, landing flat on his back.

As another big wave blasted over the deck, Lacey held on for dear life. When the water rushed back out again, he was up on his feet again, and this time no wire was going to stop him from getting to safety. He lowered his head and plowed right through, snapping the wire loose. Lacey didn't stop until he was inside the watertight door and holding on to the work table. The three of us came running into the ET (Electronics Technicians) workshop, laughing and whooping. Lacey had turned white, and was still gripping the work bench, muttering incoherently in shock.

"I ain't never, I ain't never, I ain't never going out there again. You're all assholes. Fuck you, fuck you, fuck you all. Goddamn it, I ain't never going out there again."

Lacey was shaking and we couldn't stop laughing. He was one of funniest sights we'd ever seen. Lacey was now called "Surfer Joe" for the rest of the way home, the only man capable of tube-riding a Navy ship's fantail.

After a couple of days, the shock wore off and I saw Lacey telling his great adventure to a group of guys. You could tell he was describing his adventure by all his body contortions and frantic gestures. Word of his experience spread quickly all over the ship. Guys yelled, "Surf's up," and Lacey would jump up into his best Surfer Joe tube riding position with a big smile on his face. He was elevated to hero's status and he loved every minute.

The last hurdle before entering home port was the custom's inspection and search for contraband. Guys on board had silver, gold, and various other stuff they didn't want to declare and had hidden around the ship. But the Number One item that was hidden was hashish, bought in Naples and Marseilles. It was hidden all over the ship. In the HT shop, half the lagging in the welding booth was pulled down one night and filled with pounds of hash. It was repainted and the guys welded up a storm so black welding ash would float around, covering any telltale sign of a repair job. Another secret stash spot was a new pipe that went from one small passageway to the next, each dead-heading against the bulkhead. It was a pipe starting nowhere and ending nowhere, filled with hash. There were hundreds of other ingenious hiding spots all over the ship, and even after the dope-sniffing dogs came on board, nothing was found.

The excitement was high the next morning as we pulled into Norfolk. There were hundreds of people waiting at the end of the pier. The Navy band was blowing standard military tunes and Welcome Home posters and banners could be read as we pulled in. I planned to call my friend, Brad, to ask him to bring my car down, if it was still in one piece, and we'd go have a few beers together at the beach. After the initial rush to get off the ship, I cruised on down to the end of the pier and found my surf buddies from Virginia Beach waiting for me. Wow, what a great surprise.

"It's about time you showed up, asshole. Come on, the car's packed and the surf's up at Cape Hatteras."

Now, that's the only way to end a cruise.

Chapter 21

Conclusion

As you can tell from these stories, the Navy has some very unique people. During my 22 years of naval service, I had to work for long periods of time with people I hated. It was the discipline, the perseverance, and the excellent training I received that helped me survive and cope with the knee-deep piles of shit that always seeming to flow towards me. And, considering that I was a Hull Technician, wading through knee-deep shit was just part of my job anyway.

Despite all the negative things that happened in these stories, I never regretted joining the Navy. I was able to travel to places that people only dream about, and had adventures that you only read about in books like this one. The best part of all was the people. I met more fantastic friends and had more fun than I ever thought I could, with people from all walks of life.

Being a Navy diver was one of the greatest accomplishments of my life. Without a doubt I will always feel honored and proud to say that I was a Navy diver. I would recommend Navy Special Warfare (Divers, Explosive Ordinance, and Seals) to anyone who feels they have what it takes. The craziness in this book was, in many respects, our way of coping with the stress, boredom, and living in cramped quarters.

After being out of the Navy for a few years now, I can remember the bad times, but more often, I reminisce about the friends and the good times I had. And if you enjoyed this book, just remember, this was only one of my many cruises.

About The Author

Dan Fredrickson retired from the Navy after serving 22 years and achieving the rank of Chief Petty Officer - First Class Diver. His training included First Class Diving School at the Navy Yard, Washington, D.C.; Explosive Ordinance School, Eglin Air Force Base, Fla.; Second Class Diving School, Little Creek, Va.; C-1 H.P. Welding School, San Diego, Calif.; and Hull Technician School, San Diego, Calif. Duty Stations included the USS Puget Sound AD 38 mobile repair ship where he served in the engineering department and repair department , dive locker; USS Reclaimer ARS 41 ocean-going tug and salvage ship where he served as a Hull Technician Supervisor, Dive Supervisor; Naval Submarine Diving Center where he served as a Second Class School Instructor; Mobile Diving and Salvage Unit 1 where he served as a Diver and Dive Supervisor; Explosive Ordinance Disposal 1, where he served as a Team Leader and Dive Supervisor. Dan currently lives and works in Southern California.

Navy Yard - Potomac River
Washington, D.C. - 1978
Author at 1st Class Diving School
Outside temperature 15°
Water temperature 30°

MK-5 Mod I
Mixed gas diving helmut

300 lbs. dive suit

USS Puget Sound (AD-38)

The USS Puget Sound has had a long and important history. Built by the Puget Sound Naval Shipyard in 1965, she was commissioned on April 27, 1968. She served with a standard compliment of 1420 officers and enlisted personnel until decommissioning on January 27, 1996. The USS Puget Sound is a Samuel Gompers Class Destroyer/Cruiser Tender. As an auxiliary ship, her main duties were to support combatant vessels or ships-of-the-line. Her primary mission was to fix and repair all types of equipment found onboard other U.S. naval ships. She could function as a fuel tanker, resupply ship, repair anything onboard a ship that did not require dry dock facilities, medical and dental facilities, and ammunition resupply. Her nuclear support facility had the capability of refueling nuclear vessels.

CPSIA information can be obtained at www.ICGtesting.com
Printed in the USA
BVOW042334141112

305522BV00003B/205/A